THE
SCOTTISH
COOKERY BOOK

To my mother, who taught me to cook,
and to Caroline without whom this
book would not have happened.

First published in Great Britain in 1998 by
Lomond Books
36 West Shore Road
Granton
Edinburgh EH5 1QD

Produced by Colin Baxter Photography Ltd

Photographs by Gary Baker
Colour illustrations by Zöe Hall
Black and white illustrations by Jacqueline Stevenson
© Colin Baxter Photography Ltd 1998
All rights reserved

A CIP catalogue record for this book is available from the British Library

ISBN 0 947782 71 0

Printed in Hong Kong

Front Cover Photograph: *Scotch Pancakes (p131)*
Back Cover Photograph: *Salmon with Asparagus & Chervil (p54)*
Page One Photograph: *Chicken with Red Wine & Smoked Bacon (p98), Plum Clafoutis (p114) and Dauphinoise Potatoes (p74)*

THE
SCOTTISH
COOKERY BOOK

Christopher Trotter

LOMOND BOOKS
EDINBURGH · SCOTLAND

Contents

Pigeon Salad (p42), Escalope of Salmon with Watercress (p50)

INTRODUCTION

Food from Scotland is, to me, the best there is. For hundreds of years Scotland has grown, harvested, produced and processed food that is more natural and has more flavour than food from anywhere else in the world.

The fertile soil, climate, and Scotland's long tradition of husbandry, curing and preserving methods put the country in the forefront when it comes to creating and exporting food products, some of which are the finest and most sought-after delicacies in the world.

In Scotland we have a tremendous variety of natural foods, which stem from the qualities of the landscape: superb beef, lamb and venison from the fields and hills, salmon, trout and shellfish from the abundant streams, lochs and extensive coastline; and grains, fine vegetables such as potatoes, and soft fruits from the rich, fertile soil. From these wonderful raw ingredients we have also developed a wide variety of other products, including smoked foods, biscuits, breads, jam and marmalade; and perhaps the best known of all Scottish exports – whisky.

The culinary tradition in Scotland began, as in many other countries, with cooking in iron pots over open fires, the equivalent to the French 'pot au feu' – a dish in which meat, vegetables and grain were cooked in stages in a large pot of water to produce a rich and nourishing meal. Many of these

Trout with Almonds (p65)

early cooking methods are reflected in dishes still around today, for example, 'Chicken in the Pot'. However, whereas France came to be regarded as a culinary giant, Scottish cooking seemed to lose its way. Possibly the crushing of the clan system in the eighteenth century, which led to the break-up of a way of life and its culinary traditions, was partly responsible. Perhaps it was due to the French chefs, who came over here after the French Revolution, and whose culinary influence lingers to this day. Their new masters, the lairds of Scotland, demanded the best quality cuts of meat, and many of today's terms, especially for cuts of meat, show the French influence, for example 'fillet of beef' is derived from the French 'filet de boeuf'.

So what is Scottish cooking? Although Scotland appears to lack a culinary tradition, there is a long tradition of husbandry and food production, combined with a quality of landscape and climate second to none. I maintain that if the raw ingredients used to create contemporary dishes in the home or in a restaurant, be they meat, game, fish, fruit, or vegetable are from Scotland, it is Scottish cooking. The cook or chef, inspired by his or her surroundings, and by international influences, can create wonderful new dishes, often based on traditional methods, using raw materials from Scotland. After all, what is French cooking if not born of Italian chefs 200 years ago?

My passion for cooking with Scottish food dates back to when I ran a small fishing inn on Loch Awe with my wife. I had spent some time working abroad and in England, and it was a revelation to return to Scotland and cook with the wonderful raw produce which I had taken for granted as a child growing up in Scotland. It was here, too, that I discovered the remarkable wild harvest on the doorstep: wild herbs like sorrel and wild garlic, rowanberries and fungi, and fish from the loch.

The only problem was in locating a reliable source of supply; very often I had to go to out-of-the-way places to collect produce. I remember a box of odds and ends of live fish on the quayside at Tarbert, which ended up as a fish stew; and swimming in a loch to collect oysters by hand! Today there are still problems in locating produce. Recently I ordered asparagus from a vegetable supplier, it was delivered the next day, and had come from Spain! Needless to say I telephoned the supplier to ask why, with the best asparagus in the world only 30 miles away from me, he had to buy it from Spain. Nowadays I buy direct!

This book takes a look back to see how previous generations of Scots prepared this produce; for example, how the Arbroath Smokie developed from a necessary method of preserving fish to become a delicacy sought after the world over, or how the tradition of smoking food produced a wonderful soup like Cullen Skink, or a dish such as Ham and Haddie.

These dishes remind us of the history of cooking with wonderful raw ingredients, simplicity being at the heart of all that is best in Scottish cooking. This holds good in contemporary recipes, and some of my own offerings and ideas are developments of the same raw materials used in traditional dishes, letting the excellence of the natural ingredients speak for themselves. The food needs no disguise or over-embellishment.

Here are some delicious dishes, simple to prepare, using the best of what is produced in Scotland: succulent fillet of beef, with a delicate wild garlic sauce as an ideal accompaniment; a venison steak, tender as beef fillet, but healthier and with more flavour, which needs only some brambles to show it off; or try smoked venison, with just a simple accompaniment of dauphinoise potatoes. The wonderful, firm texture of salmon, combined with asparagus and chervil, exemplifies using what is fresh, in season and readily available. What could be better than delicious fresh halibut with a simple cheese and mustard glaze? Or the wonderful, perfumed flavour of Scottish tayberries, in Tayberry Tart?

These recipes are not difficult and go somewhat against the current trend of combining complex techniques and a wide variety of ingredients, together with some technical wizardry, which seem to surround us.

Here then is a collection of recipes designed to show off what to me is the best food in the world.

Christopher Trotter
Scotland's Larder
Upper Largo, Fife

FIRST COURSES

Cock a Leekie (p12), Cullen Skink (p18) and Asparagus Soup (p17)

INGREDIENTS

1.5-2kg / 3-4 lb boiling fowl

1 onion, peeled and studded
  with cloves

10 large leeks, washed and
  trimmed

1 bay leaf

1 sprig of thyme

2 stalks fresh parsley

6 peppercorns

24 stoned dried prunes

water

2-3tbsp fresh parsley,
  chopped to garnish

SERVES 8

Cock a Leekie

A traditional soup using everything available to a farmstead, although I am not sure where the prunes will have crept in! They do, however, add a touch of sweetness and if the bird was old, which it most certainly would have been, then the sweetness of the prunes would have given the soup a real lift. The leeks also may have been bitter and would likewise benefit from the addition of prunes. A whole bird will give enough soup for 8 people. It is really a meal in itself and for the original crofters would have represented quite a feast.

Wash the chicken and pat it dry with kitchen paper. Slice the leeks into 6mm ($^1/_4$in) slices, keeping at least 2.5cm (1in) of the green part. Put the prepared onion inside the bird. Put half the leeks into a large casserole and put the chicken on top. Add cold water to cover the chicken and bring to the boil; skim away the scum from the surface and reduce the heat to a gentle simmer. Add the herbs, cover the pan and allow to simmer gently for about 2 hours, or until the bird is cooked. Top up with water as necessary to keep the bird just covered.

When cooked, remove the bird and let it cool enough to handle. Discard the herbs and peppercorns and skim off as much fat from the broth as you can. Season with salt if need be. Cut the meat of the bird into small pieces and return it to the broth, taking care to avoid any skin or bone. Add the prunes and simmer for 5 minutes.

Blanch the remaining leeks by plunging them into boiling water and cooking for a few minutes, then refresh them in cold water and drain them. This just cooks them and they keep their lovely bright colour. Just before serving, add them to the broth to heat through. I like this method as it gives you two textures of leek; one is well cooked with little colour, the other has bite and colour.

Serve each bowl of broth with three prunes and sprinkle some chopped parsley on top.

Scotch Broth

The classic Scottish soup. Originally it would have been the entire meal, consisting of a bit of everything a household produced, meat, cereals and vegetables. It is best made the day before you want it to allow all the flavours and textures to develop. A dish for the winter, best made with mutton if available, or one-year-old lamb. The vegetables should all be cut to a similar size; about 6mm (¼in) dice. Cabbage and potato can be added, depending on season and availability. Preparation should be in three stages: soaking the peas and barley in water for an hour or so; then cooking up to the removal of the lamb; then, when the lamb is cool enough to handle, returning it to the soup.

In a large pan sweat the onion in a little lard to soften, add the meat and water to cover, bring to the boil and skim off any deposit from the surface. Add the pre-soaked barley and peas, simmer for 30 minutes. Add the remaining vegetables, continue to simmer gently until just cooked. Remove the lamb bone and allow to cool, then trim off the meat, roughly chop it and return it to the soup. Discard the bones. Just before serving add the parsley.

INGREDIENTS

1kg / 2lb piece neck of mutton, or lamb trimmed of fat

75g / 3oz pearl barley, washed and drained

75g / 3oz split peas, washed and drained

1 large onion, peeled and chopped

1 large leek, trimmed and chopped

3 small white turnips, diced, or 1 medium swede, peeled and diced

3 carrots, peeled and diced

2 tbsp fresh parsley, chopped

water

SERVES 4

Watercress Soup

The vibrant green colour and peppery flavour of this soup is warming on a chilly day. It is also delicious served chilled, in which case you may need to add a little single cream to thin down the texture. Perfect for summer picnics or barbecues.

Melt the butter in a heavy-based pan and add the onion, leek and thyme, stirring to coat in butter; cook gently until soft. Add the potatoes and stir to coat with the butter. Cover with stock and simmer until soft, seasoning with salt and pepper. When nearly cooked, after about 15 to 20 minutes, add the watercress and cook briefly, for about 5 minutes. Leave to cool slightly, then purée and strain through a sieve. Serve hot or chilled, with crusty bread.

INGREDIENTS

2 bunches watercress, washed

1 onion, peeled and chopped

1 leek, trimmed and sliced, avoid the very green tops

50g / 2oz butter

3 medium potatoes, peeled and sliced

vegetable or chicken stock to cover (see p136)

1 sprig fresh thyme

SERVES 4

INGREDIENTS

375g / 15oz tomatoes,
   roughly chopped
1 medium onion, sliced
good bunch of basil
300ml / 10fl oz chicken stock
   (see p136) or stock cube
   dissolved in boiling water
15g / ½ oz butter
salt and pepper
pinch sugar

SERVES 4

INGREDIENTS

2 carcasses from cooked game
   birds, or rabbit or hare
500g / 1lb mixed game meat,
   eg venison, pheasant or
   rabbit
2 carrots, peeled and sliced
3 leeks, washed and chopped
1 head of celery, chopped
1 onion, peeled and stuck
   with cloves
1 bay leaf, sprig each of
   thyme and rosemary
125g / 4oz lean minced beef
2 litres / 3¼ pints brown stock
   (see p136)
120ml / 4fl oz sherry
150ml / 5fl oz port

SERVES 4

Tomato & Basil Soup

A real height of the summer soup, and not to be attempted with anything less than the best ripe Scottish tomatoes and fresh basil.

Melt the butter in a large pan and add the sliced onion, allow to cook gently until soft. Add the tomatoes, sugar and basil, stir to coat with butter. Cook gently, stirring occasionally, for about 10 minutes. When the tomatoes are completely soft add the stock and simmer for 3 minutes. Remove from the heat, liquidise and strain through a sieve; add seasoning if necessary.

Game Soup

An excellent way to use up game carcasses or old game birds, left over after you have had a roast, very much in the tradition of 'the pot on the fire' cooking. A tasty, powerful soup.

Chop up the carcasses, and the meat, place it all in a dish and brown well in a hot oven, 220°C / 425°F / Gas 7 for 30 minutes. Remove from the oven and place in a large saucepan with the stock, vegetables and herbs, bring to the boil and simmer slowly for about 2 hours, then strain off the liquid. Take out any pieces of game which can be chopped and added to the final soup. Let the stock get cold and skim off the fat. Return the stock to a saucepan, add the sherry and minced beef and simmer for 30 minutes, season and strain again. Add the port to this stock, and any diced game meat kept for garnish.

Ripe Scottish Tomatoes

INGREDIENTS

350g / 12oz celery stalks,
  chopped and washed

125g / 4oz potatoes, peeled
  and chopped

the white of 2 medium leeks,
  chopped and washed

600ml / 1 pint chicken stock
  (see p136)

150ml / 5fl oz single cream

150ml / 5fl oz milk

25g / 1oz butter

125g / 4oz Lanark Blue cheese

freshly ground black pepper

SERVES 4

Celery & Lanark Blue Soup

Cheese often makes a good base for a soup and is a good way of using up any leftover pieces. I love the combination of celery and blue cheese and since meeting Humphrey Errington, who makes Lanark Blue, I always make this soup with his cheese. It has a creamy quality with just enough edge to give the soup a richness which belies the small quantity of cream in it. Stilton was of course the original blue cheese, although Lanark Blue is based on Roquefort, the blue cheese from France. Lanark Blue is made with raw ewes' milk. He also makes a cows' milk cheese called Dunsyre Blue which can be used in this soup, it is not so creamy and therefore does not add that richness to the flavour.

Melt the butter in a large pan over a low heat. Add the leeks and sweat to soften, add the potatoes and coat well with the butter, cook gently for about 10 minutes, taking care not to let it colour. Add the stock, and the cheese, crumbled into small pieces. Season with black pepper. Bring to the boil and simmer gently for 20 minutes until the vegetables are soft. Remove from the heat and allow to cool, add the milk and purée to a smooth cream. Return to the stove and add the cream, heat through but do not allow to boil, check for seasoning and serve.

INGREDIENTS

1kg / 2lb parsnips, peeled

125g / 4oz butter

2 onions, peeled and sliced

2 tsp curry powder

1 tsp turmeric

1¼ litre / 2 pints chicken
  stock (see p136)

salt and pepper

SERVES 4

Curried Parsnip Soup

Melt the butter in a pan and sweat the onions gently in it, taking care not to add any colour. Cut the parsnips into even-sized pieces, add them and stir them to coat in the butter. Cover the pan and cook very gently for 5 minutes to soften the parsnips. Add the spices and seasoning, mix around, add the stock and bring to the boil. Simmer for about 30 minutes or until the parsnips are completely soft. Allow to cool a little then purée in a liquidiser.

Carrot & Coriander Soup

The spicy, almost eastern flavour of coriander really complements this earthy vegetable and the slow cooking helps to create a velvety texture. The flecks of green through the soup balance well with the bright orange colour.

Melt the butter in a large deep pan, add the sliced onions and when soft add the carrots, mix around to coat them in the butter and heat through. Add the sherry and season with salt and pepper. Cover tightly, and cook slowly over a very low heat for about 20 minutes. Add the stock, simmer until the carrots are completely soft. Add the coriander, remove from the heat, cool slightly and purée until smooth. If the soup is too thick add a little more stock or water. Check the seasoning; serve with some grated carrot on top.

INGREDIENTS

2 large onions, peeled and sliced

1kg / 2lb carrots, washed, peeled and cut into small even pieces

150ml / 5fl oz sweet sherry

150ml / 5fl oz chicken stock (see p136)

75g / 3oz butter

2 tbsp fresh coriander, chopped

SERVES 4

Asparagus Soup

This is delicious served hot or chilled and is perfect for summer picnics or barbecues. If you have some water from cooking asparagus previously then you can use that as part of the liquid.

In a heavy-based pan melt the butter and add the onion, leek and thyme, stirring to coat in butter, and cook gently. Cut off the hard bases of the asparagus and discard. Cut off the tips and put aside.

Roughly chop the middle bits of the asparagus and put into the pan and soften gently. Add the potatoes and stir to coat with the butter. Cover with stock and simmer until soft. Season with salt and pepper.

When nearly cooked after about 15 to 20 minutes, add the tips and cook briefly, for about 5 minutes. Leave to cool slightly, then purée and strain through a sieve. Serve hot or chilled. You can keep some of the tips back and use them as a garnish.

INGREDIENTS

1kg / 2lb asparagus

1 onion, peeled and chopped

1 leek, sliced

50g / 2oz butter

3 medium potatoes, peeled and sliced

vegetable or chicken stock to cover, a little over 600ml / 1 pint

1 sprig fresh thyme

SERVES 4

Cullen Skink

The name simply means an 'essence' from Cullen, a village on the north-east coast of Scotland. It is the sort of soup whose deep smoky flavour and creamy texture belie the simplicity of making. It is traditionally made with Finnan haddock, which needs to be skinned after cooking; by all means do this, but the following method is easier!

In a large pan, place the fish, milk and the bay leaf, and poach gently over a low heat, or else the milk will burn, it only takes a few minutes. Remove the fish and put in its place the onion and potato, continue to cook gently until soft. Obviously the more finely chopped the potato to start the quicker this will be. When the vegetables are soft, remove the bay leaf. Liquidise the milk and potato mixture to a smooth cream. I find that a food processor is not good enough, you need to use a liquidiser. When ready return the liquidised mixture to the pan and season, probably only with pepper. Flake the smoked fish back into the soup and serve with chopped parsley.

INGREDIENTS

500g / 1lb undyed, smoked
  haddock fillets
1 medium onion, peeled and
  sliced
900ml / 1½ pints milk
1 medium potato, peeled and
  chopped
1 bay leaf

SERVES 4

Partan Bree

A traditional soup, or 'bree', made from crabs, or 'partans'. Best to use whole crabs, but dressed crabs are fine as an alternative.

Remove the meat from the crabs and reserve the claw meat. Place rice and milk in a saucepan and cook until the rice is soft but not flabby, this will take about 15 minutes. Add the brown meat and liquidise to a smooth cream. Return the mixture to a saucepan, add the stock and bring gently to the boil, stirring all the time to prevent the crab sticking. Season and add the claw meat. At the last moment as it boils remove from the heat and add the cream; do not allow the soup to boil again after the cream has been added or it will curdle.

INGREDIENTS

2 large boiled crabs
3 tbsp long grain white rice
600ml / 1 pint milk
600ml / 1 pint chicken stock
  (see p136)
salt and pepper
300ml / 10fl oz double cream

SERVES 4

Avocado & Mussel Soup

Mussels have been a Scottish staple for centuries, along with their elevated cousins, the oysters.

Clean the mussels, by scrubbing well in cold water; using a sharp knife, scrape them to remove the 'beard'. Discard any broken ones and any which do not close when tapped sharply on the shell. Heat the olive oil in a large pan, add the onions and peppers and sweat them gently, without colouring, for 15 minutes. Skin and roughly chop the tomatoes, crush the garlic with the salt and add to the pan with the tomatoes. Simmer gently, uncovered, for a few minutes, adding the seasoning and the marjoram. Add the mussels, cover and cook for 15 minutes, when cooked, the mussels will all have opened (discard any which haven't); remove them and keep to one side. Add the water and bring to the boil. Skin and stone the avocados, chop and add to the soup. Do not cook, but just heat through and then purée. Return the mussels to the soup, either in their shells or taken out.

INGREDIENTS

1kg / 2lb mussels

2 medium onions, peeled and chopped

2 large red peppers, seeded and chopped

2 tbsp olive oil

500g / 1lb ripe tomatoes

6 cloves garlic, peeled and crushed

1 tsp sea salt

good bunch fresh marjoram

2 avocados

900ml / 1½ pints water

SERVES 4

Beetroot Soup

The Russians do not have the monopoly on beetroot soups, there are various mentions in Scottish cooking, one such made with venison stock and grated beetroot to create a consommé. This recipe is for a bolder, richer and thicker broth, which I prefer.

Heat the oil in a heavy-based pan and soften the onions in it. Add the potatoes and beetroot, stir to coat in oil, cover and cook gently for a few minutes to soften. Add the stock and bring to the boil, season and simmer gently, covered, for about 30 minutes or until the vegetables are completely soft. Allow to cool a little, then purée until smooth and velvety. Reheat and serve with a spoonful of yoghurt.

INGREDIENTS

3 tbsp vegetable oil

1 medium onion, peeled and sliced

1 clove garlic, peeled and crushed

400g / 14oz raw beetroot, peeled and sliced

2 medium potatoes, peeled and sliced

600ml / 1 pint chicken stock

salt and pepper

plain yoghurt

SERVES 4

Dressed Crab

A simple but delicious way of serving crab, taken from Theodora Fitzgibbon.

For some of the crab recipes in this book you can use a fresh crab which can be bought ready cooked at the fishmonger. He will also 'pick' it for you if you ask him nicely!

Mash the brown crab meat and half the white meat from the claws together in a bowl. Mix in the breadcrumbs, add the cream or yoghurt and Tabasco or Worcester sauce. Season with salt and pepper as required. Put the mixture back into the shell of the crab. Decorate the top with the remaining meat from the claws. Serve with crusty white bread and lemon wedges.

INGREDIENTS

1 large boiled crab

2 tbsp fresh white
breadcrumbs

a few drops Tabasco or
Worcester sauce

2 tbsp double cream or plain
yoghurt

SERVES 4

Potted Crab

A delightfully simple recipe which would grace any table. Originally a pestle and mortar would have been used to combine the butter with the crab; I find a food processor does the job just as well. Ah, the bliss of modern convenience.

Clarified butter is the yellow fat taken from butter which has been melted very slowly. When left to cool, the clarified part will solidify leaving the white milk behind.

Take all the edible white and brown meat from the crabs. Put it in a food processor, add the butter and the seasonings. Process until it is smooth, but not too fine. Press into little pots or ramekins and cover with clarified butter. It is essential to make sure the insides of the ramekins are very clean, and that no crab is visible above the butter. They will keep for several days in the fridge.

INGREDIENTS

2 large boiled crabs

125g / 4oz butter

2 tsp anchovy essence

salt and cayenne pepper

pinch of mace

3 tbsp clarified butter

SERVES 4

INGREDIENTS

25g / 1oz butter

25g / 1oz plain flour

250ml / 8fl oz fish stock (see
  p136) or milk

50g / 2oz brown crab meat

50g / 2oz white crab meat

few drops lemon juice

1 tsp tomato purée

2 tsp sherry

3 eggs, separated

300ml / 10fl oz double cream

50g / 2oz grated
  Strathkinness cheese

salt and pepper

SERVES 4

INGREDIENTS

the white and dark meat
  from 2 crabs

50g / 2oz butter

3 spring onions, finely
  chopped

pinch mace

pinch cayenne pepper

150ml / 5fl oz white wine

splash Worcester sauce

125g / 4oz medium oatmeal

10 anchovy fillets

1 egg, beaten

300ml / 10fl oz double cream

SERVES 4

Crab Soufflé

Strathkinness cheese works best in this recipe, if you are unable to find it, use Gruyère or Parmesan.

Heat the fish stock or milk. Melt the butter in a saucepan, add the flour and cook for a few minutes, stirring from time to time, then gradually add the fish stock. Cook gently for 10 minutes, remove from the heat and cool.

Add the crab meat, season and add lemon juice. Add the tomato purée, sherry and egg yolks and mix in well. Whip the egg whites stiffly and fold into the crab mixture. Pour into a buttered 1.25 litre / 2 pint mould. Cook in a bain marie in a preheated oven at 190°C / 375°F / Gas 5, until set. Remove from the oven and cool slightly.

Turn out onto an oven-proof serving dish. Pour over the cream and sprinkle the cheese on top, return to the oven and bake for about 15 minutes. Serve immediately on its own or with a salad.

Baked Crab
with Oatmeal Topping

Beat the egg with the cream, soften the butter and add to the crab. Mix in the spices, spring onions and wine. Add three-quarters of the oatmeal and 5 chopped anchovies. Put into a buttered dish and sprinkle with the rest of the oatmeal. Spread the remaining anchovies on top. Bake in the oven, 190°C / 375°F / Gas 5 for 20 minutes until puffed up and browned.

Garlic Prawns

On the west coast, prawns mean anything from a large shrimp up to a lobster, so for cooking times you will have to judge for yourself!

Plunge the prawns into boiling water and return to the boil for about a minute, remove and let the water drain off.

In a food processor purée the garlic and herbs and then add the butter, blend together and add some salt and pepper. Refrigerate for about 1 hour, until set.

Preheat the oven to about 200°C / 400°F / Gas 6. Place the prawns on a baking sheet and liberally dot the butter over them. Bake in the oven until the butter is hot and bubbling, this should take about 5 minutes. Serve the prawns on hot plates with the butter poured over.

INGREDIENTS

1.5kg / 3lb fresh prawns or langoustines
350g / 12oz butter at room temperature
2 cloves garlic
3 tbsp fresh herbs: parsley, tarragon, fennel, washed and taken off their stalks
salt and pepper

SERVES 4

Oysters

My first oysters were eaten at the home of a gourmet friend of my father's; he, along with a local restaurateur from Anstruther, got a case and the three of them consumed the lot, apart from my 12, which I enjoyed but which were quite enough for me!

Since then I have eaten oysters on the continent and in England, but I have to say that for me, the best are from the west coast of Scotland and the ones I usually go for are from Loch Fyne.

Oysters are available all year round. They are delicious either cooked or simply as they are with perhaps a squeeze of lemon juice. Oyster knives are easily available nowadays. The latest gadget is a 'clic huitres' which combines an excellent knife and a malleable plastic holder to grip them with.

INGREDIENTS

allow about 12 oysters per person
squeeze lemon juice (optional)

INGREDIENTS

60 mussels

2 large onions, peeled and
  finely chopped

125g / 4oz butter

75g / 3oz plain flour

½ bottle white wine

300ml / 10fl oz double cream

2 tsp fresh parsley, chopped

600ml / 1 pint milk

1 bay leaf

1 sprig thyme

1 small whole or ½ onion

SERVES 4

Mussel & Onion Stew

There is quite a bit of work in this recipe but the result is well worth it. A hotel near Musselburgh, whose mussel beds were known about as far back as the Romans, gave rise to this one. Today we can get superb rope-grown mussels which are without barnacles and sand, and they have a hundred times more flavour than the imported green-lipped mussels.

Wash the mussels, removing the 'beard', the bit of weed they attach themselves to the rope with, and rinse in cold water. Discard any broken or open ones which don't close when tapped sharply on the side of a pan. Put the cleaned mussels into a large pan with the wine and cover. Bring to the boil and simmer until they open, this takes only a few moments. Discard any which have not opened. Strain off the liquid and reserve. Remove the mussels from their shells and keep them on one side. Place the bay leaf, thyme and onion into a pan of milk, heat gently for about 5 minutes and strain. Keep the milk warm.

Melt the butter in a saucepan, and sweat the chopped onions in it. Stir in the flour, pour on the hot mussel juices, stirring to create a thick sauce, then add the warm milk. If the liquids are warm then no lumps will form. Cook gently so the flour loses its dry taste.

Return the mussels to the stew, add the cream and bring back to just below the boil. Mussels must not be cooked too long or they go rubbery. Serve on hot plates sprinkled with parsley, with copious quantities of crusty white bread.

Steamed Mussels with White Wine & Cream

The simplest of dishes, the difficult bit is in the preparation. Wild mussels are not a good idea nowadays unless you know exactly where they come from and are happy about how clean the water is. Farmed mussels are so good and they are generally rope-grown, which means that they are suspended in the water and do not get covered in barnacles and weed.

You need to give them a good scrub and remove the bit of weed or 'beard', which is what the mussel has used to attach itself to the rope and to its colleagues. This is done by scraping with a sharp knife. Rinse in plenty of cold water and they are ready to use. Discard any broken ones and any which do not close when tapped sharply on the shell.

Put the vegetables into a heavy-based pan, large enough to take the mussels when covered with a lid. Put in the mussels and pour on the wine.

Over a gentle heat allow the mussels to steam in the wine until they are all open. This will take about 5 minutes. Discard any which have not opened.

Remove the lid and bring to a rapid boil. Pour on the cream and return to the boil; simmer for about two minutes. Distribute the mussels between four bowls, season with black pepper and sprinkle with chopped parsley, pour over the sauce making sure the vegetables are evenly distributed. Serve immediately.

INGREDIENTS

2kg / 4lb mussels

½ onion, peeled and finely chopped

1 medium carrot, peeled and finely chopped

1 stick of celery, finely chopped

150ml / 5fl oz white wine

300ml / 10fl oz double cream

ground black pepper

1 tbsp fresh parsley, chopped

INGREDIENTS

40 princess scallops

1 sprig each of parsley and
*   thyme*

1 bay leaf

6 peppercorns

150ml / 5fl oz dry white wine

150ml / 5fl oz water

1 packet saffron

70ml / 2½fl oz double cream

2 tbsp fresh parsley, chopped

salt and pepper

SERVES 4

INGREDIENTS

16 to 20 scallops

2 leeks, trimmed

2.5cm / 1in ginger, peeled and
*   cut into fine strips*

1 tbsp sunflower oil

50g / 2oz butter

salt and pepper

SERVES 4

Princess Scallops with Saffron

It is not so easy to find fresh princess scallops but the frozen queens are just as good and cook just the same. The fresh ones should be treated like mussels (see p25) when cleaning and discarding open and broken ones.

Wash the scallops in cold water. Put the herbs and peppercorns into a pan which has a good lid, add the scallops and wine, cover and cook gently until the shells open or they are defrosted. Remove the scallops from the pan, keep them warm. Crush the saffron and add to the pan, reduce the liquid by about half and then add the cream, season and bring to a gentle boil. The sauce should have a coating texture. Remove from the heat, strain into another saucepan, add the parsley. Put the scallops into warm bowls and pour the cream sauce over them.

King Scallops with Leek & Ginger

Scottish scallops are simply the best, but as with all shellfish they must be cooked for the minimum of time, otherwise they can be rubbery. This dish combines their delicacy with the robust leek and an oriental hint with the ginger.

Wash and trim the leek, don't discard too much of the green as the colour is good in this dish, but too much can be coarse. Cut the leeks into barrels, about 5cm (2in), then cut these in half lengthways and slice thinly into strips. Carefully wash and dry the scallops with kitchen towel. Heat a heavy-based frying pan and add the oil and butter. Fry the scallops on both sides, allowing to colour slightly, they will cook very quickly. Remove the scallops from the pan, keep warm. Put the leeks into the pan and stir until they are light brown and limp. Add the ginger and season. Serve strewn over the fish.

Marinaded Mackerel (p34), Fillet of Halibut with Cheese & Mustard Glaze (p56), Princess Scallops with Saffron (p26)

INGREDIENTS

*smoked salmon (allow 50g /
2oz per person or 100g / 4 oz
for a main dish)*

sliced brown bread

lemon wedges

SERVES 4

Smoked Salmon

Smoking has been used for centuries as a method of preserving food. Today smoking is big business and it is easy to become blasé about smoked salmon since it is apparently so plentiful and relatively cheap. As a result a proliferation of 'added value products' are on the shelves to tempt us, with things like malt whisky, or Cajun spices. Beware, the true product should be lightly brined first then smoked over smouldering oak logs for between 24 and 48 hours. Most modern stainless-steel kilns can push a side through in under 8 hours. Inverawe Smokehouse in Argyll still smoke in the traditional manner; it may cost more but it is worth it.

It is worth briefly talking about the smoking process, since there are two ways of producing smoked fish.

Hot smoking is the process where the fish is smoked close to the heat source producing the smoke and is effectively 'cooked'. Cold smoking is where the fish is placed further away from the heat source in the smoker and is only bathed in smoke, and is not cooked at all. The reason the fish does not 'go off' is because it has been brined, or dipped in a salt solution, which prevents bacteria breaking down the material. In general terms hot smoked food is flaky, and cold smoked is firmer and sliceable, like traditional smoked salmon. Today there are various types of smoked salmon alongside the traditional one above, some are brined longer and some are hot smoked. Different smokehouses have different names for them, it is worth reading the small print.

To serve

If you buy smoked salmon in vacuum packs, open them at least half an hour before you want to serve the fish, to allow it to 'breathe'. In my opinion smoked salmon should be served with good brown bread (see p126) and unsalted butter with a wedge of lemon, if you insist, good salmon does not need the latter. The flavour is clean, not salty, with the fresh fish flavour balanced by the depth of oak smoke. The texture should be firm and not flabby or oily.

Gravadlax

The name is certainly not Scottish, but Scandinavian. However, we do have long connections with Scandinavia, not least with the Vikings. The only bit which may be slightly out of context is the use of dill – I am not sure how native it is!

Gravadlax is in many ways like smoked salmon, which is also brined, but with smoked salmon the brining is the process before the smoking whereas in this dish the brining is the main part. This is of course what prevents the fish going off. It is essential to use the freshest fish possible and although some people say frozen fish is perfectly good, I believe the texture alters, and that nothing but the best, freshest salmon will do – which of course means Scottish, or better still, from Shetland, which has deeply Scandinavian roots.

Mix together all the dry ingredients. On a plastic tray big enough to take the salmon, sprinkle a third of the mixture. Place one side of salmon skin-side down on it; sprinkle with another third of the mixture. Make sure that the whole fish is covered. Place the second side of salmon on top, with the skin facing up and sprinkle the rest of the salt mixture over the top. Cover with cling film and place a weight on top, of about 1kg (2lb). Put it into a cool place or the fridge. After 2 days turn the whole 'sandwich' over and baste with the moisture which will have been exuded. The gravadlax will be ready in about another day. Scrape off any excess salt and slice the salmon either like smoked salmon or in the Scandinavian way in wedges almost straight down. Serve with a dill mustard (see p138).

INGREDIENTS

2kg / 4lb piece of salmon, filleted, but not skinned, this weight is without the head and the tail cut off a good 10cm (4in) up.

4 tbsp coarse salt

4 tbsp granulated sugar

2 tsp coarsely ground black pepper

6 tbsp fresh dill, roughly chopped

SERVES 4

Smoked Fish Platter

An assortment of smoked fish, presented on a plate, makes a superb main dish, and a good talking point.

Suggested smoked fish:

Smoked salmon As in the recipe on page 28, cold smoked, served thinly sliced.

Kiln-roasted salmon This is hot-smoked and usually comes in steaks.

Cold-smoked trout This is farmed rainbow trout grown to several pounds in weight and then smoked like salmon, it has a lighter flavour and texture than salmon, but is very good in its own right. Inverawe produce a smoked Loch Etive trout which is fish-farmed in Loch Etive.

Hot-smoked or kiln-smoked trout These are whole trout, about 250g (8oz) size; the flesh is flaky and they are usually sold whole. They come apart easily by removing the skin, which just peels away, then the four fillets will lift off if you take a knife down each side to loosen.

Smoked mackerel royale An unusual product unique to J.C. Morris of St Monans in Fife. The mackerel is cold-smoked then very thinly sliced.

Smoked mussels Hot-smoked, serve as they are.

Smokie This a haddock which has been smoked whole and is hot-smoked. It is generally served cold, but can be served warm. Traditionally from Arbroath, or more accurately from Auchmithie; there is little or no fishing now from Auchmithie, but there is a little restaurant there called the 'But 'n Ben' which is well worth a visit.

Oysters Hot-smoked and delicious! Arrange small quantities of each of these on the plate, serve with lemon wedges, plenty of good brown bread and butter and a little creamed horseradish, this is especially good with hot-smoked trout, lemon-flavoured mayonnaise is also good, or even dill mustard (see p138). A meal fit for a king!

INGREDIENTS

Small portions of each
smoked salmon
kiln-roasted salmon
cold-smoked trout
hot-smoked trout
smoked mackerel royale
smoked mussels
Arbroath smokie
oysters

SERVES 4

Hot- and Cold-Smoked Fish

INGREDIENTS

4 small undyed, smoked
   haddock

a little water

4 slices of smoked ham

2 tbsp butter

5 tbsp double cream

black pepper

SERVES 4

INGREDIENTS

2 kippers

4 tbsp plain yoghurt

butter

pepper

lemon juice (optional)

SERVES 4

Ham & Haddie

This recipe exemplifies the tradition of fine combinations of simple ingredients producing something greater then the sum of the parts.

Poach the haddock in the water, remove them and keep warm, don't let them dry out. Heat the butter in a frying pan and gently warm the ham through, then place the ham on top of the haddock. Pour the haddock juices into the pan the ham was in, add the cream and simmer gently, seasoning with black pepper. Pour the liquid over the ham and haddock and put briefly under a hot grill. Serve immediately.

Kipper Pâté

Kippers, which are brined and smoked herrings, are a true Scottish delicacy, but so often poorly represented, and not given the treatment they deserve. They can be salty and dry but at their best can be plump, moist, rich and sweet. The most famous is a Loch Fyne kipper, but there are probably more kippers about called Loch Fyne than there are herring in Loch Fyne!

Cooking a kipper without the smell getting onto everything is simple. Butter a sheet of tin foil and place the kipper on top. Put a few more dots of butter on the fish and fold in the foil. Bake in a medium oven, 190°C/375F/Gas 5 for about 15 minutes and that's it.

To make the pâté, let the kippers cool in the foil, then remove all the bones. Put the kippers into a food processor with the seasoning and lemon juice, whizz to a purée. Add the yoghurt and whizz to combine. Check for seasoning and add lemon juice if required. Press into ramekins and chill for at least 6 hours or overnight. Serve with toast.

Loch Etive Trout Caviar

I do love this product and I think Inverawe Smokehouses smoke the best salmon; they also produce this 'caviar' which is large trout roe prepared like sturgeon's roe; it is smaller and a brilliant orange colour but quite delicious served with sour cream and toast. Cut the toast in fingers and put a teaspoon of soured cream on, with a teaspoon of caviar, and enjoy!

INGREDIENTS
Loch Etive trout caviar
  (allow 50g / 2oz per person)
toast
sour cream

Arbroath Smokies

These are smoked haddocks which were originally prepared in Auchmithie, a tiny fishing village on the cliff edge just north of Arbroath, overlooking the North Sea. The fishwives would gut, lightly salt and hang the haddocks over hot smoke from oak or birch chips. This gives the fish a mild smoke, and a sort of tanned colour. Smoked in this way the moisture is kept in and the flesh keeps its pale colour.

There is now a sea fish festival at Arbroath and they are trying to make sure the appellation 'Arbroath' is always used with the fish. I must say I cannot see anyone else trying to steal it – Kennoway Smokie does not have the same ring!

To grill an Arbroath Smokie
Brush the fish with melted butter and put under a hot grill for about 2 minutes, this helps to loosen the bone. Open up the fish by slitting it down the backbone, and lifting out the bone, which will come away easily. Brush again with butter and put back under the grill to heat through.

Very good hot with a baked potato; it is also excellent served cold.

INGREDIENTS
4 Arbroath Smokies
125g / 4oz butter

SERVES 4

Marinaded Mackerel

INGREDIENTS

4 mackerel, filleted and
boned
2 tbsp olive oil

Marinade

2 tbsp fresh coriander,
chopped
2 tbsp fresh parsley, chopped
1 tbsp fresh chives, chopped
1 clove garlic, crushed
1 tbsp runny honey
150ml / 5fl oz olive oil
150ml / 5fl oz white wine
vinegar

SERVES 4

This is not the only recipe in this book for mackerel, which is a much underrated fish. It is cheap and relatively plentiful. Some people find them rather oily, but to me this is a bonus; the oil provides flavour and makes mackerel perfect for grilling since they need no extra fat; surely one of the most heavenly smells is that of mackerel on a grill. Oiliness can also be combated by using good combinations; no cream but lemons or dry wine. They must be eaten fresh, their blue-black skin shimmering in the light. If you cannot eat them immediately then this recipe is for you.

Ask your fishmonger to fillet and bone the fish for you, or you can buy them already done, but it is preferable to see the fish whole, and look for the bright skin and full clear eyes.

First make the marinade; combine the oil and wine vinegar with the honey and whisk together, add the crushed garlic and then the fresh herbs. Leave to sit for about 1 hour.

Wipe the fish clean, and using a sharp knife make 2 or 3 slashes down the skin side. Heat a frying pan and add 2 tablespoons olive oil. Fry the fish, skin side down, very quickly, until browned a little; the slashes will help to stop the fish from curling in the heat, cook quicker and look good as the colour of the flesh shows through the skin. Turn the fish over and cook it on the other side, the whole process will take about 5 minutes. Put the fillets on a tray, and whilst still hot pour the marinade over them and leave to cool for at least 6 hours before serving. These are delicious served cold with a potato salad, (see p143).

Sea Kale with Cheese

An unusual vegetable grown by the Pattullos in Glamis but becoming more widely available. The Scottish variety is available in February and can be eaten raw with cheese or with dips. It is excellent in salads and with butter sauce (see p137).

This simple recipe is especially delicious with Strathkinness, a nutty flavoured cheese from Dundee.

Trim the sea kale, taking off the dirty bases, and wash gently in cold water.

In a double boiler steam the sea kale for 4 minutes to take away the hard crunch, but leaving a 'bite' for texture. Arrange the stems evenly on warm plates and sprinkle the cheese over the pale green fronds, season and serve immediately.

INGREDIENTS
*a good bundle of sea kale,
   about 350g / 12oz
125g / 4oz finely grated
   Strathkinness cheese
salt and pepper*

SERVES 4

Tomato, Basil & Goats' Cheese

This idea, I admit, is one I got while working in France, but today we now have all the main ingredients required; the only other one is olive oil and the best comes from Italy. Crottins are small goats' cheeses, available in the summer months from Arran or Gigha.

Slice the tomatoes thinly horizontally. Slice the crottins the same way, they are harder to do, so cut maybe three slices from each and break each slice in two.

Switch on the grill for at least 5 minutes before use. Arrange the cheese, tomatoes and basil leaves in little piles on plates with the basil under the cheese and finish the pile with cheese. Season each layer as you go. Sprinkle each plate with a good splurge of olive oil and flash under the grill until the cheese starts to bubble. Serve immediately.

INGREDIENTS
*4 plump ripe Scottish
   tomatoes, blanched and
   peeled
2 crottins
12 basil leaves
salt and pepper
really good virgin olive oil*

SERVES 4

INGREDIENTS

Roulade

750g / 1½lb fresh spinach

50g / 2oz butter

½ tsp grated nutmeg

4 eggs, separated

75g / 3oz Strathkinness
  cheese, grated

Sauce

1 onion, peeled and finely
  chopped

250g / 8oz wild mushrooms

50g / 2oz butter

25g / 1oz plain flour

150ml / 5fl oz double cream

SERVES 4

Spinach Roulade with a Wild Mushroom Sauce

This is good enough to have in place of meat any day. The rich vibrant green of spinach with a lovely creamy mushroom sauce is a fine combination. If you can't be bothered to wash and blanch fresh spinach, then frozen will do.

Line a 30.5cm x 21.5cm (12in x 8½in) baking sheet with greaseproof paper. Wash the spinach and remove the stems. Blanch by placing it in boiling salted water for 2 minutes and refreshing immediately in cold water. Drain. If using frozen spinach, let it defrost completely before use.

Squeeze out the excess water from the spinach, and chop in a food processor. In a large pan melt the butter and add the spinach to dry it out further, add seasoning and nutmeg. Remove from the heat, allow to cool. Beat the egg yolks and mix them into the spinach.

In a large bowl whisk the egg whites with a pinch of salt until stiff; whisk a third into the spinach mixture to loosen it, then return it all to the bowl of egg whites, folding it in carefully with a plastic spatula to retain the air. Spread the mixture onto the baking sheet to cover it and bake at 180°C/350°F/Gas 4 for 15 minutes.

Sprinkle another sheet of greaseproof paper with the grated cheese. Turn out the roulade onto the prepared paper and cover with a damp cloth, leave to cool.

Melt the butter in a pan and add the onions, cook gently to soften. Wash and slice the mushrooms and add them to the pan. Cook gently for a few minutes and then add the flour. Stir gently to avoid breaking up the mushrooms, add the cream and bring to the boil. Season. Spread this mixture onto the roulade and roll it up carefully. Return it to the oven for 3 or 4 minutes to just warm it through, and serve.

Spinach Roulade with a Wild Mushroom Sauce

INGREDIENTS

250g / 8oz shortcrust pastry

5 large onions

115g / 4oz butter

150ml / 5fl oz double cream

2 eggs

Creamy Onion Tart

Onions are full of natural sugar and it is amazing how sweet they can be. The best ones for this dish are young firm ones, not too big, those huge Dutch things are so full of water that when they cook down they almost disappear to nothing. This dish does need patience to get a rich flavour and colour but is well worth it.

Peel and finely chop the onions, try to keep them as even a size as possible, this gives the dish a uniformity. Melt the butter in a wide-based frying pan, which you can also cover, it does not need to be a lid, but you have to cover it enough to keep some heat in. Add the onions and over a high heat sweat them, then stir around in the butter, once mixed cover the pan and allow the onions to exude some steam. After 4 minutes remove the lid and reduce the heat a little. Continue to stir and cook gently, stirring occasionally, for up to 45 minutes, this allows the natural sugar to come out. As the water evaporates, the onions begin to colour lightly brown. When they reach this stage pour in the cream and allow to simmer for a few minutes to thicken, then remove the pan from the heat and add salt and pepper. When cool mix in two beaten eggs.

Line a 20cm (8in) metal flan case with the pastry and bake blind. When the pastry is cool pour in the onion mixture and bake in the oven, 220°C/425°F/Gas 7 for 15 minutes until set and lightly browned.

Serve hot or warm on its own for a first course or with a salad for a light supper dish.

Winter Salad

There are no fresh leaves to speak of in Scotland in the winter months, the colourful mixed bags you can get from the supermarkets, which don't have much flavour, can however provide a base for something of a bit more colour and flavour.

Finely chop the red onion. Cut the leek into fine strips and blanch by plunging them into boiling salted water for 1 minute, then strain them and refresh them immediately in cold water to cool. Dice the cheese into small cubes. Remove the outer leaves of the cabbage and cut the core out, wash and shred the leaves finely.

Poach the quails' eggs. This is a lot easier than you might think! You need a shallow pan of simmering water with a dash of vinegar, an egg cup, a slotted spoon, a bowl of ice-cold water, a plate and some kitchen paper. Using a thin knife gently break the shell of the egg and open it up gently into the egg cup. Carefully lower the cup into the simmering water allowing some water to cover and firm up the egg, then let it slide into the water and cook for about 2 minutes, the white should change from opaque to just white. Lift the egg out with the slotted spoon and put it straight into the cold water to stop the cooking. Repeat with all the eggs and when they are all cooled lift them out of the water and dry them on the paper. This last bit can be done just before you assemble the salad since the quails' eggs will keep in cold water for a couple of days.

Combine the salad ingredients and add your favourite dressing, and then place the quails' eggs on the top.

INGREDIENTS
mixed lettuce leaves
½ red onion, peeled
2 tsp pine nuts
8 quails' eggs
75g / 3oz St Andrews cheese
¼ red cabbage
½ leek

Asparagus with Chervil Butter

Scottish asparagus is a little-known delicacy, but the Pattullos in Glamis have won national awards for their superb quality spears and I commend it to you.

Peel the asparagus with a potato peeler, gently working from just below the tender tip to the base; wash the spears and trim the bases off evenly to give about 10cm (4in) lengths, use the rest for soup. Bring the water to the boil, add the salt and plunge the asparagus into it. Cook for about 7 minutes or until you can just spear a stem with a knife and it slips out easily. Put on one side and keep it warm.

Put the asparagus water into a small pan. Chop half the chervil, add it to the water and reduce the liquid by half. Add the cream and bring to the boil. Away from the heat swirl in the butter, return the spears to the pan and add the lemon juice and season, heat through but do not boil. Place the spears on four plates and pour the sauce over the tips. Strew the remaining chervil over the top.

INGREDIENTS

40 medium asparagus spears
1 litre / 1³/₄ pints water
15g / ¹/₂oz coarse salt
4 tbsp asparagus water
265g / 8¹/₂oz cold butter, cut in pieces
salt and pepper
3 tbsp chervil sprigs
salt and pepper
1 tbsp lemon juice
2 tbsp double cream

SERVES 4

Steamed Asparagus

There is a lot of worry about cooking asparagus, and there are all sorts of complex and expensive gadgets for cooking it. I prefer to simply boil it in salted water and serve with melted butter.

Peel the asparagus as for the asparagus with chervil butter, (above) but only cut off the bottom 2.5cm (1in) or so. Fill a large pan, big enough to hold the asparagus easily, with water and add the salt. Bring to a rolling boil and plunge the asparagus in. Don't overcrowd the pan, it may be best to cook it in two batches. Bring back to the boil, simmer for 5 minutes; check that a knife will slide easily out of the stem about halfway up. Drain and let them steam dry, taking care not to damage the tips. Serve on warm plates with melted, unsalted butter.

INGREDIENTS

24 asparagus spears
sea salt
175g / 6oz unsalted butter, melted

SERVES 4

Fine Scottish Asparagus Spears

INGREDIENTS

2 young mallards

nut oil

220g / 7oz fat bacon

350g / 12oz wild duck livers,
* if available, or make up*
* with chicken livers*

2 tsp salt

½ tsp ground black pepper

pinch each of ground cloves,
* nutmeg and ginger*

250ml / 8fl oz double cream

4 egg yolks

2½ tbsp brandy

50g / 2oz sultanas

SERVES 4

INGREDIENTS

4 pigeon breasts

salt and pepper

1 tbsp butter

a selection of salad leaves

herb leaves, eg sorrel, chervil
* and tarragon*

Dressing

125ml / 4fl oz olive oil

30ml / 1fl oz white wine
* vinegar*

1 tsp wholegrain mustard

pinch sugar

2 tsp sunflower seeds

SERVES 4

Terrine of Duck

This terrine takes two days to prepare; the first day to roast the bird and leave it to rest overnight, the next day to make the terrine and refrigerate it overnight.

Preheat the oven to 250°C / 475°F / Gas 9. Remove the legs from the ducks. Season the birds and sprinkle with oil. Roast them for 15 minutes, let them cool and leave to rest, overnight if possible.

Put the fat bacon, livers, salt, pepper and spices into the food processor and blend to a smooth, creamy consistency. Add the egg yolks, cream and brandy. Continue to blend for about 30 seconds. Push the mix through a sieve. Rinse the sultanas in warm water and dry on kitchen paper. Remove the breasts from the ducks and skin them. Cut them into small pieces. Mix them and the sultanas into the liver mixture. Put the mixture into a terrine or an earthenware bowl, cover and cook in a bain marie for 30 minutes at 200°C / 400°F / Gas 6. Allow to cool, and refrigerate overnight. Serve with toast.

Salad of Pigeon

Melt the butter in a heavy-based pan and as it foams, season the pigeon breasts and place them skin-side down in the pan for 2 minutes to brown and seal. Turn them over and lower the heat. Cover partially and lower the heat for 2 minutes, then remove from the heat, leave in the pan to rest for at least 5 minutes.

The salad leaves should be in 'bite-size' pieces and mixed with the dressing, and add some large-leafed herbs like sorrel. Arrange the salad in the centre of each plate. Take the pigeon breasts from the pan; they should still be warm. Place them, flesh-side down, on a board and remove the skin. Slice them thinly top to bottom and arrange the slices around the salad. Put the pan back on the heat and toss in the sunflower seeds to lightly colour them then drizzle them over the pigeon, fleck with a few small herb leaves and serve.

Main Courses

Fish Stew (p58)

INGREDIENTS

1kg / 2lb fresh salmon

2 shallots, peeled and
  chopped

1 tbsp chives, chopped

salt and pepper

pinch of mace

150ml / 5fl oz water

150ml / 5fl oz dry white wine

125g / 4oz mushrooms,
  chopped

1 tbsp fresh parsley, chopped

SERVES 4

Tweed Kettle

Salmon is one of the major ambassadors abroad for Scottish produce; it is sought after in the world's best markets and recognised as being the king of fish. This is usually applied to the wild variety which was fished in abundance from the rivers Tay, Awe and Tweed to name but three. It was once so plentiful that there was a law preventing the owners of estates from feeding their staff on salmon more than three times a week! Today it is a little different. Wild salmon is harder to come by, and is probably still better than the farmed variety, but since the wild fish swim the Atlantic and back feeding on a varied diet its superiority is not surprising. However, I believe that properly sourced farmed salmon is a fine product, the best coming from the Shetland Islands where their strict regulations and strong seas create a fish as close to a wild one as you will get.

This traditional recipe is from Edinburgh. It was a very popular dish in the nineteenth century, sold in cookshops and inns in the city, with mashed potatoes. The sauce can be thickened with egg and cream, but it is not traditional.

Put the salmon in a pan which it fits neatly, add water to just cover and poach the fish gently for about 5 minutes. Remove from the pan and reserve the cooking liquor. Remove all the skin and bone, add them to the liquor and simmer for 10 minutes. Strain and reserve the liquor. Cut the fish into cubes about 5cm (2in) across. Season with salt, pepper and mace. Put into a clean dish with 150ml (5fl oz) of the fish liquor, wine and shallots. Cover and gently simmer for 10 minutes.

Meanwhile heat up the butter and stew the mushrooms gently in it for 2 or 3 minutes, add the chives, drain off the liquid and add to the salmon. Serve strewn with the chopped parsley and with mashed potatoes.

Cold Salmon

A cold poached whole salmon makes a classic centrepiece of a buffet. However, I believe that baking the fish or part of a fish whole is a better method which keeps the flavour and moisture in. This idea is simple but you do have to be quite brave with timing and get to know your own oven. I once read of a recipe for cooking a whole fish in a dishwashing machine! You can imagine the dinner-table discussion, instead of talking about the relative merits of Neffs and Agas it would be Mieles or Hoovers! You may have to adjust the cooking time, depending on the size of the fish.

Heat the oven to 160°C / 325°F / Gas 3. Take a piece of foil big enough to wrap the fish and pour 2 teaspoons of olive oil, to cover the sheet, where the fish will sit. Rub the fish with olive oil and seasoning and stuff the cavity with the herbs.

Wrap up the fish quite loosely in the foil and bake in the oven for an hour. To check if it is cooked, unwrap it and push it lightly on top, if it is firm it is cooked, if slightly springy, then it isn't. Another way to check if it is cooked is to make sure no blood is visible on the bone inside the cavity. Either allow the salmon to cool quickly and refrigerate or serve warm with one of the sauces suggested later on, (see pp137-139).

INGREDIENTS

1.5kg / 3lb salmon, cleaned
  and scaled
2 tsp olive oil
salt and black pepper
1 bay leaf
8-10 sprigs of thyme
8-10 fresh parsley stalks

SERVES 4

Salmon Steamed in Seaweed

INGREDIENTS

1 whole salmon, cleaned and
* scaled*
1kg / 2lb seaweed
1 bottle of light red wine

SERVES 4

I first met this method of cooking in France when I was working in a restaurant in Obersteinbach in the Alsace region. In spite of the fact that we were miles from the sea we worked with a lot of good fish. Eel was something of a local delicacy and we got a lot of live ones to deal with. A customer had just flown in from fishing on the River Tay and he brought a superb salmon into the kitchen, it must have been taken from the water that morning and was quite dazzling. All the cuisiniers crowded round to marvel at this magnificent fish and I basked in the reflected glory. They had never seen such a fish; what they didn't know was that neither had I!

You can get seaweed either from the fishmonger or gathered from rocks from a safe and clean beach, bladderwrack or dulse is best, don't use the old stuff washed up beyond the tide, but the fresh bright-looking weed still attached to rocks. Give it a good rinse to get rid of sand and crawly beasties!

You need either a roasting tray or dish which the salmon will fit into, a fish kettle will do fine. If the salmon is very large, then remove the head and tail, but it looks good served whole.

Place a trivet or cooling rack in the tray and cover it with seaweed. Place the fish on top, and cover with seaweed. Pour over the red wine. Either steam over a low heat on the top of the cooker or put in a medium oven, 180°C/350°F/Gas 4 for about 30 minutes, basting regularly with the red wine. It is difficult to be precise about times, but if you look inside the cavity there should not be any sign of blood along the backbone. When cooked, take a little of the liquor and use it instead of the vinegar to make a butter sauce (see p137).

Remove all the seaweed from the salmon and slide it carefully onto the serving dish; brush it with a little oil to keep it shiny. To serve, cut along the side of the fish, peel off the skin and cut chunks from the bone. The smell of the sea and the moisture is wonderful.

INGREDIENTS

250g / 8oz cold cooked
*   salmon, flaked*
2 tbsp plain flour
2 eggs
150ml / 5fl oz double cream
salt and cayenne pepper
2 tbsp vegetable oil

Sauce

125g / 4oz melted butter
2 tbsp double cream
2 tsp plain flour
2 tsp soy sauce
2 tsp mushroom ketchup

SERVES 4

INGREDIENTS

escalopes of salmon (allow
*   3 x 50-75g / 2-3oz escalopes*
*   per person)*
salt and pepper
good bunch of watercress
150ml / 5fl oz dry vermouth
75g / 3oz butter
2 or 3 tbsp double cream

SERVES 4

Salmon Fritters

A traditional way of using up leftover pieces of fish from a whole steamed or baked one.

Mix the flour, beaten eggs and cream into the salmon to create a soft mixture, you may not need all the cream. Season to taste. Heat the oil in a pan and drop in tablespoons of the mixture, fry until golden brown on both sides, then drain on kitchen paper. Keep warm.

For the sauce, mix the cream with the flour and add to the melted butter in a pan, stirring all the time. When combined add the soy and ketchup, and mix in. Serve with the fritters.

Escalope of Salmon with Watercress

A simple dish which makes use of the naturally growing watercress; if you do gather it from the wild, make sure that it is from free-flowing water and not too close to major agricultural activity. The colour of the sauce provides a lovely backdrop for the delicate pink of the salmon.

Remove the stalks from the watercress, wash the leaves and chop them quite finely, this can be done in a food processor.

In a heavy-based pan melt the butter, season the salmon with salt and pepper and place in the pan. Heat gently until just cooked, turn over to finish the other side; it takes about 30 seconds each side. Remove the fish and keep it warm. Add the vermouth and chopped watercress to the pan and allow to bubble gently; reduce the liquid by half, then add the double cream. Check for seasoning. You want a lightly coating texture but not too thick. Spoon some sauce onto each plate then place the salmon on top. Serve immediately.

Salmon in Pastry

In a small pan with a good lid, designed for the oven, cook the onion over a low heat in a little butter until translucent. Add the rice and stir to coat in the butter. Add the stock, bring to the boil and add the bay leaf. Cover the pan, place it in the oven, 180°C/350°F/Gas 4 for 20 minutes. When the rice is cooked, gently fluff it up with a fork and leave to cool.

Finely slice the mushrooms and fry them in butter for 2 to 3 minutes. To assemble, roll out the pastry to a square, long enough for the fish, with 2.5cm (1in) of pastry free at each end. Sprinkle half the rice in a strip across the centre of the pastry. Cover this with one fillet of salmon, moisten it with a little wine and season. Place half the sliced egg and mushrooms on top of the salmon, repeat the process with the other fillet, wine and seasonings. Continue with the other layers, finishing with a layer of rice. Fold the pastry over the fish, using an egg wash to make it stick. Decorate with pastry trimmings and brush over with eggwash.

Leave the salmon parcel to rest in a cool place for about 1 hour, then bake it in a hot oven, 220°C/425°F/Gas 7 for about 40 minutes. If the pastry browns too fast, then turn the heat down.

Serve with a lemon butter sauce or wild garlic sauce (see pp138 and 139).

INGREDIENTS

1kg / 2lb approx. piece of boned salmon, giving 2 fillets

175g / 6oz button mushrooms

3 eggs, boiled until just firm, sliced

1 small onion, peeled and finely chopped

175g / 6oz long grain white rice

450ml / 15fl oz light stock eg fish or chicken (see p136)

1 bay leaf

500g / 1lb puff pastry

1 tsp butter

2 tbsp white wine

1 egg, beaten

SERVES 4

Salmon Steak with Chanterelles

I love this dish, it represents all that is best about Scottish food: the abundance – salmon is plentiful; the richness – it is known as the king of fish! The simplicity – who needs to mess about when the food speaks for itself? – and the hunter gatherer – chanterelles are beautiful orange-yellow mushrooms shaped like trumpets whose smell is evocative of the moss-laden woods you find them in. This is an almost shamefully simple recipe, but not quite.

First, gather the chanterelles. These should preferably not be washed; if you have collected them yourself, cut the base off and gently clean away any pieces of moss or leaves still clinging. Keep the small ones whole but slice the larger ones through the middle, they will cook more quickly. If you have bought them, gently wash them, and pat dry on kitchen paper. Cook them as soon as possible after washing.

Heat half the butter in a heavy-based pan, until it just melts. Carefully place the salmon escalopes in, making sure none overlap; cook gently on each side for 2 or 3 minutes. Remove and keep warm. Raise the heat and add the chanterelles, cook quickly and allow the heat to soften them. Add the stock and a little butter. When the liquid has nearly gone, take the pan off the full heat. Swirl the rest of the butter in to thicken the sauce. Serve with the salmon fillets overlapped on the plate with the chanterelles on top.

INGREDIENTS

salmon steaks (allow 3 x 50g / 2oz pieces per person)
75g / 3oz butter
125g / 4oz chanterelles, prepared
125ml / 4fl oz chicken stock
salt and pepper

SERVES 4

Salmon Steak with Chanterelles and Loch Fyne Gigas Oysters (p23)

INGREDIENTS

salmon escalopes (allow
  3 x 50g / 2oz per person)
2 tbsp fresh chervil, chopped
asparagus spears (allow 5
  per person)
150ml / 5fl oz dry white wine
150ml / 5fl oz fish stock (see
  p136) or water
300ml / 10fl oz double cream
75g / 3oz butter
squeeze lemon juice
  (optional)

SERVES 4

Salmon with Asparagus & Chervil

Salmon is known as the king of fish, and rightly so because of its strength and endurance so it should, by rights, have some magnificent cooking companions.

This dish, like so many, is a development and I owe a debt to Alan Holland at Mallory Court Hotel in Warwickshire for the idea of combining chervil and asparagus, I have combined them with the salmon. This is only a dish for someone you really love!

You need to cut slices of salmon from a side which has been boned, so that you get pieces of about 50g (2oz), a bit thicker than smoked salmon slices.

In a wide, heavy-based pan, cook the salmon very gently in the butter, turn over to complete the cooking, it will take about 30 seconds on each side. Remove the salmon and keep it warm.

Add the wine and fish stock if you have it, but water is fine, bring to the boil. Add the asparagus, and simmer until cooked. Remove the asparagus with a slotted spoon and keep it warm. Raise the heat and reduce the liquid by half, stirring all the time, and then add the cream. Add the chopped chervil to finish. The sauce should be of a texture to coat the back of a spoon. You may want to add a squeeze of lemon juice.

To serve, spoon the sauce onto the plate, place the salmon in the middle of each plate and arrange the asparagus tips around the edge, nose to tail at an angle.

INGREDIENTS

500g / 1lb sole fillets

5 tbsp white wine

1 leek, carrot and celery
stick, washed and cut into
thin strips about 5cm / 2in

pinch saffron

6 tbsp double cream

salt and pepper

SERVES 4

INGREDIENTS

4 halibut steaks, each
175g / 6oz

210g / 7oz Strathkinness
cheese, grated

3 tsp wholegrain mustard

60ml / 2fl oz double cream

salt and pepper

SERVES 4

Fricassée of Sole

The chief thing to remember when cooking fish is not to overcook it. This dish is so quick it can be cooked while guests are at the table.

Cut the sole into strips of about 8cm (3in). Blanch the vegetables in boiling salted water and refresh in cold water to keep them lightly crisp and to retain their brilliant colour.

Poach the fish in the white wine, this only takes moments. The fish will turn from translucent to white; remove the pieces with a slotted spoon, add the pinch of saffron, the cream and the vegetables, simmer gently until a coating texture is achieved then return the sole to the pan. Season and serve.

Fillets of Halibut with a Cheese & Mustard Glaze

Butter the base of an oven-proof dish. Place the fish, skin-side down, in the dish and season with salt and pepper.

Mix the grated cheese and mustard together, with enough cream to form a spreadable but thick paste. Season with salt and pepper. Spread the mixture evenly over the fish. Bake in a hot oven, 200°C/400°F/Gas 6, for 20 minutes.

The topping will be browned and bubbling with the lovely flaky fish underneath.

Devilled Pike

Scottish lochs are renowned for their salmon and trout fishing but many of them have all sorts of other fish such as eels and pike. Sadly few are brought out as they are not much appreciated. Loch Awe has a fine representation; we ran the Portsonachan Hotel on the shores of the loch for 5 years and in that time a few were brought to the kitchen. Some of them we had smoked at Inverawe by Robert Campbell-Preston, which was interesting, but never caught on. The most frightening was a 9kg (18lb) fish, which was brought into the kitchen one afternoon. It was huge, with what seemed like rows of tiny sharp teeth, and eyes which stared accusingly at you without proof! I had never seen a pike before, let alone one of some 9kg (18lb)!

It is not the easiest fish to prepare but a much underrated one and this recipe will soon liven it up. I love the name because most pike are devils and to cook it in its own sauce so to speak is very satisfying.

Season the flour with the salt and pepper and put it on a plate. Cut the fish into bite-size pieces and dust them in the flour. Heat a frying pan with the oil and fry the pieces until crisp and lightly browned. Put the remaining ingredients in a saucepan and add the fish. Bring to the boil and simmer gently for 15 minutes. Serve with pilaff rice (as in kedgeree – see page 61).

INGREDIENTS

750g / 1½lb pike meat or
  other white fish

2 tbsp plain flour

salt and pepper

4 tbsp olive oil

175ml / 6fl oz white wine
  vinegar

4 tbsp blossom honey

1 clove garlic, crushed

1 small onion, peeled and
  chopped

½ tsp mace

1 tsp curry powder

SERVES 4

INGREDIENTS

1 large onion, roughly chopped

1 leek, roughly chopped

1 tbsp olive oil

1 clove of garlic, crushed

250g / 8oz ripe tomatoes

1 tsp tomato paste

500g / 1lb fish bones, washed
  and cleaned of any blood

piece of orange peel

salt and papper

parsley stalks, bay leaf, fennel

water to cover

150ml / 5fl oz white wine

approx. 1kg / 2lb fish eg,
  fillets of salmon cut in
  chunks, scallops, mussels in
  the shell, white fish cut in
  spoon size pieces etc.

4 tomatoes, blanched, peeled
  and cut in quarters with the
  pips removed

SERVES 4

INGREDIENTS

4 whole mackerel

4 sticks of rhubarb

50g / 2oz brown sugar

4 tbsp olive oil

salt and pepper

2 tsp wholegrain mustard

SERVES 4

Fish Stew

Heat a large pan with some olive oil, add the onion and sweat, add the leek and sweat until soft. Add the garlic and tomatoes and cook for 5 minutes. Add the fish bones, orange peel, herbs, the white wine and tomato purée and bring to the boil, then add the water to cover and bring to the boil; skim off the scum, season and simmer for 30 minutes. Stand the soup aside to cool, then strain it by pushing the juices through a sieve with the back of a ladle.

Bring the liquid back to the boil and add the fish, firm varieties first, shellfish last. Thus salmon, cod and halibut, then sole and plaice, then mussels and scallops. Bring back to a gentle simmer, then poach everything briefly for about 2 minutes. Remove from the heat, add the tomato quarters to heat through and serve on hot plates with copious quantities of chopped parsley.

Mackerel with Rhubarb Relish

The oily flavour of this magnificent fish is foiled superbly by this ubiquitous vegetable.

Trim the rhubarb and cut into 2.5cm (1in) pieces, wash and shake dry. Place it in a pan with a well-fitting lid, sprinkle on the sugar and add the wholegrain mustard. Stew gently over a low heat with the lid on for about 30 minutes, until the rhubarb is completely soft. Stir to really combine, set aside and keep warm.

Turn on the grill and allow to heat up for at least 5 minutes. Line the grill pan with tin foil. Using a sharp knife, slash the fish 2 or 3 times down each side, season and brush with olive oil. Place in the grill pan and grill each side for about 4 minutes until cooked. The slashes will open up to speed cooking and the skin should brown lightly. Serve on hot plates, either with the relish in ramekins or as a dollop on the side of hot plates.

Mackerel Fillets with Tomatoes, Olives & Capers

I can't resist the colour and power of this dish, a real summer stunner. Best made with really ripe tomatoes, and with olives either in herbs or fresh, definitely not in brine.

First prepare the tomatoes. Cut out the core and with a sharp knife cut a cross at the bottom of each one. Plunge them into a pan of boiling salted water for about 10 seconds, longer if they are very firm. Remove with a slotted spoon and put them immediately into a bowl of cold water to stop them cooking. Leave them there to cool completely. Remove from the water and peel off the skin. The tomatoes should be firm but the skin should peel off easily. Cut them in quarters, remove the pips and then cut each quarter in half. Set aside.

Roughly chop both the olives and capers. Slash the mackerel fillets two or three times down each side and season.

Heat a large pan and put in the olive oil, when it is hot place the mackerel in, skin-side down. Cook for about 3 minutes, then turn them over and lower the heat. When cooked, which will take another 3 minutes, remove the fillets and keep them warm. Add the capers to the pan and stir about to soak up the flavours, then add the olives and stir to heat through. Season with salt and pepper and raise the heat, add the tomatoes and toss to thoroughly mix through. Do not cook for long or else the tomato will disintegrate.

To serve, arrange the tomato mixture in the centre of four hot plates and place the mackerel, skin-side up, on top. Sprinkle with fresh chopped parsley.

INGREDIENTS

4 mackerel fillets

500g / 1lb ripe tomatoes

2 tbsp black olives, stoned

1 tbsp capers

2 tbsp olive oil

salt and pepper

2 tbsp fresh parsley, chopped

SERVES 4

Smoked Haddock with Mashed Potatoes & Spinach

This is not so much a recipe but a series of combinations. The pale yellow, cream and green look great together and the strong flavours are just sublime.

Cook and mash the potatoes with plenty of milk and butter for a smooth consistency. Poach the fish in a little water, just enough to come half way up. Set the fish aside, reduce the liquor by half, add the cream, season and simmer until it just begins to coat the back of a spoon. Take a large frying pan and heat with the butter, as it foams put all the spinach in and stir to coat and cook, take care as it may spit; season and cook to soften the leaves.

To serve, warm a big dish and place the mashed potato on one side with the fish beside it and put the spinach next to it. Pour the sauce over the fish.

INGREDIENTS

4 undyed smoked haddock fillets
water
8 tbsp double cream
500g / 1lb potatoes
1kg / 2lb fresh spinach, washed
2 tbsp butter
salt and pepper

SERVES 4

Kedgeree

This has connotations of the Indian Raj, but it was a Scottish regiment who introduced it to India and then it found its way back home. Curry powder as such does not exist in India.

Sweat the onion gently in the butter and add the rice, stir to coat with the butter. Add the stock, bring to the boil, add the bay leaf and cover, cook in a medium oven, 180°C/350°F/Gas 4 for about 20 minutes until the rice has absorbed all the stock. Meanwhile poach the fish in milk for 5 minutes. Chop the hard-boiled eggs. When the rice is cooked, use a fork to stir in the flaked fish and other ingredients, this prevents the rice from breaking up. Finally, add, about a teaspoon of curry powder; it is a matter of taste, but you must add some!

INGREDIENTS

50g / 2oz butter
1 small onion, peeled and chopped
350g / ¾lb long grain white rice
750ml / 1¼ pints chicken stock
1 bay leaf
2 fillets of smoked haddock
300ml / 10fl oz milk to poach
4 eggs, hard-boiled
1 tsp curry powder

SERVES 4

Smoked Haddock with Mashed Potatoes & Spinach

INGREDIENTS

750g / 1½lb monkfish tails,
  skinned and boned

6 ripe tomatoes

3 tbsp olive oil

salt and pepper

good bunch basil leaves

1 tbsp butter

SERVES 4

Collops of Monkfish with Tomatoes & Basil

Tomatoes and basil are a very special combination and go well together in all sorts of recipes. Here is another of my favourites, which is very simple and quick to make.

To prepare the tomatoes, cut out the core left by the stalk and with a sharp knife, cut a cross at the top of each one. Plunge them into a pan of boiling, salted water for about 10 seconds; remove with a slotted spoon and put them immediately into a bowl of cold water to halt the cooking process. Leave them there until cool. Remove from the water and peel off the skin. Cut the tomatoes in quarters, remove the pips and then cut each quarter in half. Set aside.

Slice the monkfish into chunks about 1cm (½in) thick, wash them, dry in kitchen paper and season. Heat a frying pan, add 2 tablespoons olive oil and when hot quickly cook the monkfish pieces, browning on both sides. This only takes a few minutes. Remove the monkfish and add the other spoon of olive oil if needed. Reduce heat and add the tomatoes, stir and season; at the last minute before serving, roughly tear the basil leaves and add them, and then remove from the heat, swirl in the butter to create a liaison. To serve, spoon the tomato mixture on four plates and place the monkfish pieces round it.

Herrings Fried in Oatmeal

Herring is very much a Scottish fish; whole communities lived or died because of it and groups of fishwives would move around the coast to where the herring were being landed. Such was the season, and the sheer quantity brought in, that as often as not the fish were preserved, salting and smoking being the main ways, so they could keep for the months when there were no fish, or so they could be transported. The kipper is the best-known smoked version of the herring.

Some of the most delicious meals are the simplest to prepare and the healthiest to eat, and yet very few people eat them any more. Herring, like mackerel, is an oily fish, and has a magnificent flavour, some prize it higher than salmon. This recipe combines it with another Scots staple, oatmeal; it absorbs cholesterol and therefore not only is the combination magnificent, it is also very healthy. It is important to get the right sort of oatmeal and of course the fish should be fresh. The Aberfeldy Watermill produces superb oatmeal, I would use their medium-ground variety.

Using a sharp knife, slash the sides of the fish twice, season with salt and pepper. Fill a plate with the oatmeal and roll each fish in it to coat well. Heat a frying pan and add the oil and butter, as the butter melts add the fish and cook on each side until crisp and brown, this will only take a few minutes. Drain the fish on kitchen paper and serve hot with a wedge of lemon.

INGREDIENTS

8 fresh herrings, scaled,
 cleaned and heads removed
125g / 4oz medium oatmeal
salt and pepper
1 tbsp vegetable oil
75g / 3oz butter
lemon wedges

SERVES 4

INGREDIENTS

4 trout, cleaned and splayed
  open
125g / 4oz medium oatmeal
1 tbsp vegetable oil
75g / 3oz butter
250g / 8oz gooseberries
25g / 1oz brown sugar

SERVES 4

Trout in Oatmeal with Gooseberries

This is not a traditional recipe but the sharpness of the gooseberries provides a perfect foil for the oily trout. The oatmeal is not necessary but does 'gel' very well with the sauce, probably not a good recipe for a really fine fresh brown trout, but it is very good with a rainbow trout; the latter are not indigenous to Scotland but were brought in from Canada because they farmed well, which the natural brown trout does not. Any rainbow trout found in lochs will have originated from escapees from the fish farms.

To make the sauce, trim the the gooseberries and cook them very gently in a little water with the sugar, in a small pan; a purée will form which will have some texture and pieces of gooseberry.

Meanwhile season the trout; if you want to try boning a whole one, simply take a gutted trout and press the open belly down on to a board, push firmly down the backbone and then turn it over. The bone should lift out quite easily. You can also buy the trout ready boned.

Coat both sides of the fish with oatmeal. Heat a pan with the oil and add the butter, as it foams place the trout in flesh-side down and cook on a high heat for 2 minutes, until the oatmeal is lightly coloured. Turn down the heat and after another 2 minutes turn the trout over and cook for a further 4 minutes at a lower heat. When cooked, serve with the sauce on or beside it.

If the trout are to be cooked in batches, make sure that the pan has no burnt oatmeal left in it, as this will mar the flavour.

Trout with Almonds

Brown trout are the indigenous trout to Scotland, their beautiful black-brown flecked skin helps them to hide in the peaty shallows of Scottish rivers and lochs. They have been a delicacy for many years, even Queen Victoria gave them approval, as they were taken from one of the streams on the Balmoral estate.

I can remember as a child going to the Pitlochry Festival Theatre and eating this dish and loving it. Then it was the native brown trout, beautifully flecked, pink-fleshed fish. You can still get brown trout if you fish for them, but generally it is the farmed rainbow which is more commonly available.

Sprinkle the trout on both sides with salt and pepper. Heat the oil and half the butter in a large pan, allow it to foam up, then place the trout in the pan. Cook for 2 minutes, lower the heat and cook for another 2 minutes, then turn the fish over. It should be lightly browned, if not cook it a little more before turning it over. Spoon some of the butter and oil from the pan over the fish from time to time. When cooked, there should be no sign of any blood in the cavity along the backbone. Remove from the pan and keep warm.

Add the rest of the butter to the pan, and the flaked almonds and cook gently, stirring regularly, until the almonds are golden brown. While they are cooking, place the trout on a serving dish; squeeze the lemon juice over the almonds and as it foams up in the pan, pour them over the fish. Serve sprinkled with copious quantities of parsley.

INGREDIENTS

4 whole trout, cleaned and
  kept whole
salt and pepper
1 tbsp vegetable oil
125g / 4oz butter
75g / 3oz flaked almonds
juice of ½ lemon
2-3 tbsp fresh parsley, finely
  chopped

SERVES 4

Game Casserole

INGREDIENTS

*a brace of pheasant, grouse
or other game birds, and
their livers; older birds are
preferable*

*1kg / 2lb rump steak,
trimmed of all fat*

half a hare, cut into 4 pieces

*1 large onion, peeled and
sliced*

*250g / 8oz button
mushrooms, cut into
quarters*

2 tbsp tomato purée

1 bottle red wine

2 tbsp olive oil

50g / 2oz butter

40g / 1½oz plain flour

2 cloves garlic, crushed

2 bay leaves

5 sage leaves

4 whole cloves

juice and zest of 1 orange

2 tbsp rowan jelly

water as required

salt and pepper

SERVES 8

This recipe, like most, has developed over the years. It came originally from an English chef, but in many ways it is a sort of home-coming, because the best game comes from Scotland. Once you get to know this recipe you can experiment with other meats. It is best made a day ahead.

Wipe the game birds dry with kitchen paper. Heat half the oil in a heavy-based pan and brown the birds on all sides; remove the birds and put them into a deep casserole. Brown the hare in the same way. Cut the steak into cubes, add the rest of the olive oil to the pan and brown the steak too, then add it to the casserole, along with any juices.

Melt the butter in the pan and brown the onion, add the mushrooms and garlic. Stir in the flour and season. Add all the other ingredients and bring to the boil, simmer gently and scrape any sediment off the bottom of the pan, then pour it onto the meat in the casserole. If it does not quite cover the birds then top up with water until it does.

Cover with a lid and cook in the oven, 170°C/325°F/Gas 3 for about 1½ hours, or until the birds are tender. Remove the birds and hare and let them cool enough to handle. Remove the skin from the birds and discard. Take the meat off and cut it into chunks slightly larger than the rump steak; return the meat to the casserole.

If you have the livers, cut them into small dice, quickly fry them in butter and add them to the casserole. Simmer the whole lot again and check seasoning and consistency; if it is too thin simmer gently to reduce the liquid slightly.

This casserole is best served the day after it is made, with lots of mashed potato and kale.

INGREDIENTS

2 rabbits

2 tbsp vegetable oil

90g / 3¹/₂oz streaky bacon,
 diced

10 baby onions or shallots,
 peeled and kept whole

salt and pepper

2 tbsp fine oatmeal

210ml / 7fl oz white wine

12 prunes, stoned and soaked
 in water, with a dash of
 whisky if liked

6 juniper berries

1 bay leaf

salt and pepper

SERVES 4

Rabbit with Prunes

Rabbits are plentiful in Scotland and easily obtainable, if you know a friendly farmer, rabbits are always being shot and the farmer may be happy to give them away, or only charge a few pence for them, and wild rabbit has a lovely depth of flavour. The supermarket ones are not really the same as they tend to be a bit bland. This recipe is ideal for either sort, since the prunes give a lovely sweetness to the dish.

If the rabbits have not been jointed already, cut them into four; 2 legs and 2 pieces from the saddle. Season the oatmeal and roll the rabbit pieces in it. Heat a frying pan and add the oil; brown the rabbit pieces on both sides, then remove and put to one side. In the same pan, brown the bacon and remove it, then add the onions and colour a little over a gentle heat. Put the rabbit, bacon and onions in a stew pan.

Over a gentle heat add the wine to the frying pan and, using a wooden spoon, scrape up the bits and juices from the bottom. Add the water and bring to the boil, add the bay leaf and juniper berries. Pour the liquid into the stew pan and top up with enough water to just cover the rabbit. Bring to the boil and cover, simmer gently for 40 minutes, or until the rabbit is tender.

Remove the rabbit and onions from the pan and set them aside. Put the prunes into the pan and boil rapidly until the cooking liquor thickens a little. Check the seasoning, and then remove the bay leaf and juniper berries. Return the rabbit to the pan, heat through and serve.

Jugged Hare

There are two kinds of hare in Scotland, the brown hare and the blue or mountain hare which changes its coat to white in the winter, and is more common in the Highlands. Whilst they are responsible for some crop damage they are not a real farming nuisance and they seem to be becoming rarer all the time. The meat is superb, lean and full of flavour, a real treat.

This is a traditional recipe, with very little alteration. The sophistication of the dish shows this was one for the laird and probably not the ordinary man, although I am sure that many a hare would have ended up in the pot! You need to make it a day ahead, to allow the meat to marinade overnight.

First prepare the marinade and put the pieces of jointed hare into the marinade, leave overnight.

Put the oil and butter in a large pan, over a good heat. Dry the hare on kitchen paper and fry the pieces until brown on all sides. Put the hare into a casserole which has a well-fitting lid.

Fry the bacon in the pan, then add the celery and onions, stirring to soften. Add more butter if the pan is dry. Stir in the carrots, sprinkle in the flour, and mix well to combine. Pour in some of the water, add the rowanberry jelly to create a thick porridge; let it come to a simmer then add the herbs. Pour the mixture into the casserole, stirring it through the hare. Add a little more of the water to the pan to scrape up any juices from the bottom and add them to the casserole. Add the rest of the water and top up with strained marinade, season with salt and pepper. Cover and cook in the oven at 160°-175°C/325°-350°F/Gas 3-4 for about 3 hours, or until tender.

If you prefer to make this using a whole hare, joint it, by dividing the saddle into four and each hind leg in two, giving 10 pieces including the 2 forelegs. Put them into the marinade overnight. You can use the blood of the hare to thicken the sauce at the end of cooking, instead of flour.

INGREDIENTS

1 hare, jointed
125g / 4oz butter
4 tbsp vegetable oil
175g / 6oz bacon, diced
1 head of celery, washed and
  sliced
4 medium onions, peeled and
  sliced
4 medium carrots, peeled and
  sliced
1 tbsp parsley, chopped
2 tsp thyme, chopped
2 bay leaves
3 tbsp rowanberry jelly
  (see p141)
150ml / 5fl oz port
1 heaped tbsp plain flour
900ml / 1½ pints water
salt and pepper

Marinade

3 tbsp olive oil
150ml / 5fl oz red wine
2 tbsp red wine vinegar
2 shallots, sliced
6 juniper berries, crushed
1 sprig rosemary
2 bay leaves
salt and pepper

SERVES 4

INGREDIENTS

2 saddles of hare

2 tsp olive oil

Marinade

600ml / 1 pint red wine

1 carrot and 1 onion, cut into
   small dice

1 bay leaf, 1 sprig each of
   rosemary and thyme

salt

8 peppercorns

8 juniper berries

2 cloves

The sauce

350g / 12oz cooked beetroots,
   sliced thinly

2 tbsp shallots, chopped

2 tbsp wine vinegar

210ml / 7fl oz double cream

1 tsp mustard

chives, chopped

SERVES 4

Saddle of Hare with Beetroot

Sadly there aren't too many hares around any more but if you do get the opportunity to get one then this is a superb method of cooking it. The traditional jugged hare (see p69) is to me less exciting, but none the less a fine method of preparation. This needs to be made a day ahead, to allow the meat to marinade.

With a flexible knife, remove and discard the membrane covering the saddles. Marinade the saddles with the wine, vegetables, herbs, salt, peppercorns, juniper berries and cloves for about a day.

Take the saddles out of the marinade, and dry carefully. Strain the marinade through a sieve, retain.

Heat the olive oil in an oven-proof pan, brown the saddles all over, then put them into a hot oven, 250°C / 480°F / Gas 9 for 10 to 15 minutes. They should be cooked but still pink. Leave in a warm place to rest. Remove most of the fat from the pan and cook the beetroot in it, add the shallots, cook for 2 minutes to soften.

Add the wine vinegar and 4 tablespoons of marinade. Reduce for a minute, add the cream, mustard and seasoning, and reduce until a coating consistency is achieved. Keep warm.

To serve, remove the fillets from top and bottom of the saddle and slice them lengthways, arrange them on four plates, with the beetroot sauce on top. Sprinkle with chopped chives.

Roast Venison

Venison is such a good meat and not made nearly enough of. This wonderful recipe is traditional in that it uses a marinade; today it is less necessary to marinade the meat since the quality of venison available is so high it does not need tenderising. However, in this instance it does help to provide a rich sauce.

For the marinade: cook the onions and carrots gently in the olive oil, without colouring and put into a large non-metal container which will hold the venison. Add the other ingredients. Put the haunch in and leave for two days, turning regularly to coat all sides.

When ready, remove the haunch and dry with kitchen paper. Put a large casserole, into which the haunch will fit with a lid, onto a high heat and add the oil and butter. Brown the bacon and then add the haunch, browning it all over. While doing this, in another pan reduce the marinade by half by boiling it rapidly and then strain it over the haunch. Cover and cook in the oven, 170°C/ 325°F/Gas 3 for 30 minutes per 500g (1lb).

When cooked, remove the haunch, and keep it warm, covered in foil so that it does not dry out. Strain off the juices into a pan and set to boil rapidly. Make a beurre manié by mixing the flour and butter together and then whisking into the boiling liquor. Simmer until the sauce is reduced by half, it will thicken up, add the port and the rowanberry jelly, check for seasoning and serve.

A haunch looks splendid presented at the table, if you feel confident about carving it. The less brave can take slices in advance and serve with a little sauce over the top to keep the meat moist and hot. Serve the rest of the sauce separately.

INGREDIENTS

1 haunch venison, about
*   3kg / 6lb*
2 tbsp olive oil
salt and pepper
2 tbsp butter
250g / 8oz bacon, diced

Marinade
1 bottle red wine
2 cloves garlic, crushed
1 bay leaf
2 carrots, peeled and sliced
1 onion, peeled and sliced
10 black peppercorns
1 sprig rosemary
2 juniper berries
4 tbsp olive oil

The sauce
150ml / 5fl oz port
1 tbsp rowanberry jelly (see
*   p141)*
1 tbsp butter, softened
1 tbsp plain flour

SERVES 10

Wild or Farmed Venison with Brambles

I use both farmed venison and wild venison for this dish. The wild generally comes in steaks which I buy from Rannoch Smokery. They get their meat either locally from Rannoch Moor or from Speyside, but they buy carefully and constantly check the condition and quality of the meat. With wild venison you do have to be sure about its age and condition. Farmed venison, on the other hand, guarantees a certain quality though, as with salmon, the best is never as good as the best wild, but you can be sure that it will always be good. The Fletchers produce their fine quality venison in the hills above Auchtermuchty in Fife.

Venison is a traditional meat; deer have roamed the hills for centuries, and the kings of Scotland used stay at Falkland Palace in Fife to go hunting. Traditionally they would roast a whole beast; this dish is slightly more economical and makes use of the ingredients available from the wild.

Dry the steaks on kitchen paper and season them.

Heat a heavy-bottomed pan and add a little oil and butter. When the pan is hot, put the steaks in and colour them on both sides, this seals in the juices. Cook until pink, this will take about 5 minutes, turning them again if the side facing down gets too dark. Remove the meat from the pan and keep it warm.

Add the bramble wine, the rowanberry jelly and stock or water. Bring to the boil. Stir to melt the jelly, add the brambles and as the sauce reduces and thickens whisk in the remaining butter, do not let the sauce boil again.

Serve the venison with the sauce poured over it.

Wild or Farmed Venison with Brambles
and Carrot & Coriander Soup (p17)

INGREDIENTS

4x 200g / 6oz venison steaks

2 tbsp rowanberry jelly
  (see p141)

50g / 2oz butter

4 tbsp bramble wine

sunflower oil

2 tbsp game stock or water

fresh brambles, if available

salt and pepper

SERVES 4

INGREDIENTS
slices smoked venison

Gratin Dauphinoise
850g / 1¾lb potatoes
2 tsp salt
black pepper
270ml / 9fl oz milk
125ml / 5fl oz double cream
1 clove garlic, crushed
125g / 4oz Strathkinness
  cheese, grated
olive oil

SERVES 4

Smoked Venison with Dauphinoise Potatoes

A modern 'auld alliance' dish made with superb smoked venison, some of the best comes from the Rannoch Smokery, served with rich creamy slices of potato. I think the best cheese to use in this recipe is Strathkinness, which is made at the Howgate Dairy near Dundee. It is made in large rounds and in flavour and texture terms it is a cross between Gruyère and Jarlsberg. It is perfect to use in place of Parmesan. Gratin Dauphinoise are named after the French equivalent of the Prince of Wales, the Dauphin was the king's eldest son.

Peel and slice the potatoes, but don't wash them. Lightly dry them. Put them in a pan with the milk, salt and crushed garlic and heat gently, mixing them well together over a low heat. Cover and allow to simmer gently, taking care they do not stick.

When the potatoes begin to exude their starch the milk will thicken; add the cream and continue to stir, just to coat. Bring back to the boil and then pour into an oven-proof dish. Spread the potatoes out evenly and sprinkle the cheese on top. Bake in a medium oven, 190°C / 375°F / Gas 5 for 40 minutes. They should be brown and bubbling.

Serve slices of smoked venison with a splash of good olive oil and a generous helping of Dauphinoise.

Pheasant Wrapped in Bacon with Chestnuts

Pheasant is not native to Scotland, but it is such a delicious bird and really very cheap. The season for pheasant is from October to February but the best time is from November to January. For roasting, the best birds are the young hens; for casseroling older birds will have more flavour. I personally don't like to hang them for too long; it all depends on the outside temperature and age of them, so ask your butcher's advice; a basic rule of thumb is the older the bird, especially if it is a cock, the longer the hanging required, up to 12 days.

Pheasant is not easy to roast as you need to cook the legs well but keep the breast pinkish, and it dries out so easily. I prefer this simple dish which keeps the moisture in, and you can use smoked bacon to add a touch of the exotic.

Wrap each piece of pheasant in bacon and secure with a cocktail stick.

Fry the pieces in the oil and butter in a large pan to give a little colour to the bacon.

Remove the pieces and place in a casserole dish. Add the onion to the pan and brown it a little. Add the red wine, stock and chestnuts to the pan, bring to the boil and then add to the casserole; top up with stock or water to cover the pheasant.

Cook for about 1 hour in a medium oven, 190°C/375°F/Gas 5 until tender. Remove the cocktail sticks and serve.

INGREDIENTS

2 pheasants, cut into 8 pieces
8 bacon rashers
1 tbsp vegetable oil
75g / 3oz butter
1 medium onion, chopped
150ml / 5fl oz red wine
game or chicken stock to
* cover (see p136)*
180g / 6oz dried chestnuts,
* soaked overnight*
cocktail sticks

SERVES 4

INGREDIENTS

2 young grouse

6 rashers bacon

150ml / 5fl oz red wine

1 sprig rowanberries or
 ¹/₂ lemon

50g / 2 oz butter

2 tbsp rowan berries
 (optional)

salt and pepper

1 tsp rowanberry jelly
 (see p141)

salt and pepper

SERVES 4

Roast Grouse
with Rowanberries

There is a lot of mystique about grouse, and the start of the shooting season in August used to have such ceremony. Today the ceremony has almost gone but the mystique and expensive image of grouse remain. They are delicious game birds, and a real treat. This recipe is a combination of my own ideas and a traditional one.

Wipe the grouse and place them in a roasting tin. Place the rashers of bacon over the breasts of the birds. If you have sprigs of rowanberries then place one in the cavity of each grouse as well as a little seasoned butter. Roast in a hot oven, 200°C/400°F/Gas 6 for 10 minutes, then remove the bacon and pour in the wine. Return to the oven for 10 minutes, baste the birds with the juices and cook for another 5 minutes. Remove the birds from the pan and keep them warm. Add a little water to the pan and a teaspoon of rowanberry jelly, simmer this gently until the jelly melts. Strain into another pan, add the rowanberries, and simmer until the sauce just begins to thicken. Check the seasoning.

Grouse is traditionally served on toast with bread sauce and game chips but with this sauce some skirlie is all you need (see p145). You can serve the whole bird if you like because it is traditional, but you can make it easier for your guests by simply slicing the breasts off and serving them alone on the plate, with the sauce. The legs can be used for soup or stock.

Sirloin of Beef with Wholegrain Mustard

What can one say about Scottish beef, except that at its best, it is the best. The recipes for the 'prime' cuts are simple and without much adornment, with usually only one basic accompaniment, but that is all it needs. Like Laurel and Hardy, Morecambe and Wise; you never got The Two Ronnies, a producer, two makeup artists, a stagehand and the cameraman, did you?

In this recipe I have used wholegrain mustard. Scotland does not have a tradition of mustard, but it is easy to make and there are one or two Scottish-made brands available.

A word here about drying meat before cooking it; it is essential to dry meat before fast-cooking it, as then a skin forms immediately, thus keeping the juices in the meat. If it is wet at all, the first few seconds in the pan will dry off the moisture, reducing the heat and allowing some of the juice to escape.

Heat a large frying pan and add the oil and butter. Dry the steaks with kitchen paper and season. When the butter is melted place the steaks in, brown them quickly on both sides to seal in the juices, then lower the heat and cook to your liking. I prefer rare, which takes about 1 minute on each side after sealing. Sit them on the fat side for a minute to cook the fat well – there is nothing worse than uncooked beef fat!

Take the steaks out and leave to rest, keep them warm. Lower the heat, pour off any excess fat, put in the mustard and stir in to take up the juices, then pour in the cream. Check the seasoning, and serve with the steaks.

Sirloin of Beef with Wholegrain Mustard,
Rhubarb Tart (p111) and King Scallops with Leek and Ginger (p26)

INGREDIENTS
4 sirloin or rump steaks
salt and pepper
1 tbsp vegetable oil
25g / 1oz butter
4 tsp wholegrain mustard
4 tbsp double cream

SERVES 4

INGREDIENTS

1kg / 2lb rump steak, cut very thinly

12 oysters

6 rashers thin streaky bacon

salt, pepper and cayenne

3 shallots, peeled and finely chopped

50g / 2oz plain flour

300ml / 10fl oz beef stock

250g / 8oz puff pastry

1 egg, beaten

SERVES 4

Musselburgh Pie

Musselburgh was the Roman oyster centre in Scotland and both mussels and oysters were sold on the streets of Edinburgh until relatively recent times. The oyster beds of the Firth of Forth were commented on favourably in the eighteenth century. These were native oysters and could only be eaten in the months without an 'R', the reason being that from May to August, oysters spawned and did not make good eating. Today, largely due to the work done by Loch Fyne Oysters on the west coast, Pacific or Gigas oysters are successfully farmed and we now have a year-round supply of them. Sad to say that, although we now have the availability, tastes change and the general image of the oyster has become élitist. The popular image of how they should be eaten is misconstrued and as such it gets bad press.

This should not be! If the idea of a raw oyster does not appeal to you, then this is a good way to try them, who knows you may develop a taste! This recipe is traditional and although simple, the combination of the meat and oyster is excellent.

Beat the pieces of steak as thin as possible by covering each piece with cling film and hitting it with a rolling pin. You want to end up with pieces 5cm (2in) wide and 7.5 to 10cm (3 to 4in) long. Cut the oysters in half and wrap each piece up, first in a strip of bacon, then in a strip of beef, and shape them to prevent the oysters falling out.

Sprinkle the shallots into a pie dish. Season the flour with salt, pepper and cayenne then roll the meat in it and place in the pie dish with the seam side down. Pour over the stock.

Roll out the pastry, dampen the edges of the pie dish and place the pastry over the top. Brush with egg wash and leave to rest for 30 minutes before cooking. Bake in the oven, 230°C / 450°F / Gas 8 for 15 minutes then lower the heat to 180°C / 350°F / Gas 4 for 1¼ hours. Cover the top of the pastry with foil if it is getting too brown.

Beef Olives

As one of my sources states, this dish combines economy and imagination, attributes so often found in Scottish cooking.

Trim the beef slices of any fat or gristle, cut them into strips about 15x10cm (6x4in) then, using the cling film and rolling pin method from Musselburgh Pie (see p80), flatten them out more. Mix the breadcrumbs with the onion, lemon zest, herbs, egg yolks and seasoning until well combined. Put a spoonful of the mixture on each piece of meat, roll it up and fix with a cocktail stick. Season the flour and roll the beef olives in it.

Heat the oil in a pan and brown the olives, then put them side by side in a casserole dish. Add the stock and bring to the boil. Cover and cook in the oven at 180°C/350°F/Gas 4, for about 1½ hours.

INGREDIENTS

12 thin slices of raw
  lean beef
125g / 4oz breadcrumbs
1 medium onion, peeled and
  chopped
grated zest of 1 lemon
1 tbsp parsley and marjoram,
  chopped
2 egg yolks
salt and pepper
2 tbsp vegetable oil
3 tbsp plain flour
600ml / 1 pint beef stock
cocktail sticks

SERVES 4

Sauté of Beef with Wild Mushrooms

The mushrooms should be wiped, but preferably not washed, trim away any mud or dried moss. Cut into even pieces but not too small. Some chanterelles can remain whole.

Dry the meat on kitchen paper. Heat a large frying pan and put in 2 tablespoons olive oil. Put the meat in to the pan and quickly colour it on both sides. Do not crowd the pieces, it is better to cook two batches or else the meat could poach rather than fry. Remove the meat, which should still be very rare, and put it aside, keeping it warm; add the remaining olive oil and lower the heat. Stir in the garlic and shallots, stir for about 1 minute, then raise the heat and add the mushrooms, season and cook until they just start to soften. Add the wine, bring to the boil and add the cream, as the liquid thickens, return the beef to the pan and heat through. Away from direct heat swirl in the butter. Serve on warm plates, sprinkled with chopped parsley.

INGREDIENTS

125g / 4oz mixed wild
  mushrooms
3 tbsp olive oil
2 rump or fillet steaks, cut
  into strips
salt and pepper
1 clove garlic, crushed
1 shallot, peeled and finely
  chopped
4 tbsp white wine
4 tbsp double cream
1 tbsp fresh parsley, chopped
25g / 1oz butter

SERVES 4

Fillet of Beef with Caramelised Shallots

INGREDIENTS

4 fillet steaks

1 tbsp vegetable oil

2 tsp butter

salt and pepper

20 shallots, peeled

1 tsp caster sugar

150ml / 5fl oz brown stock
(see p136)

SERVES 4

The intense onion flavour with the sweetness of the caramel make a perfect backdrop for this tender melt-in-the-mouth beef.

Heat a frying pan and add the oil and butter. Dry the steaks, season and seal them all over in the hot oil to keep the juices in, then reduce the heat a little and cook as you like them. Remove the steaks from the pan and keep them warm. Put the shallots into the pan and brown them gently on all sides, then add the sugar and stock. Cover the pan and over a gentle heat cook the shallots, they should be just cooked, but still with a good texture by the time the stock evaporates, leaving a caramelised coat in which to roll the shallots, they will be beautifully brown and shiny. Serve with the steaks.

Collops in the Pan

INGREDIENTS

8 collops of beef
(6mm- / ¼in-thick slices of
fillet steak)

1 tbsp vegetable oil

75g / 3oz butter

4 medium onions, peeled and
sliced

salt and pepper

1 tbsp pickled walnut juice;
if you cannot get pickled
walnuts, use mushroom
ketchup or even a touch of
anchovy essence, but it
won't be the same!

SERVES 4

This is another example of using a simple cooking method to show off good basic ingredients, allowing the quality of Scottish beef to speak for itself.

In a heavy-based pan brown the onions in half the butter, you need a high heat and to turn them over constantly with a wooden spoon. Reduce the heat and cook for 10 more minutes to soften. Remove the onions from the pan and keep warm. Wipe the pan out and put in the rest of the butter. Wipe the collops dry with kitchen paper, and when the butter is foaming put the collops in, colour them on both sides, this takes about 4 minutes; remove from the pan, return the onions to the pan, heat through and add the walnut juice. Season with salt and pepper. To serve, arrange the onions in a mound on the base of a plate, with the steaks on top.

Collops in the Pan

INGREDIENTS

4 fillet steaks
salt and pepper
1 tbsp vegetable oil

The sauce
2 tsp butter
1 tbsp white wine
2 egg yolks
175g / 6oz butter, melted
15 wild garlic leaves
lemon juice (optional)

SERVES 4

Fillet of Beef
with Wild Garlic Sauce

The basis of this recipe is a hollandaise sauce. When I was on Loch Awe, the spring brought amongst other wild foods an abundance of wild garlic; the smell hit you before you got there. The beautiful, elegant long green leaves grow thickly in wet ground and in summer produce tiny white flowers. Use the leaves for this recipe. The sauce can be made on its own, it is good with fish or lamb, too.

Heat a frying pan and add the oil and butter. Dry the steaks, season and cook as you like them. Make sure that you seal them all over first in the hot oil to keep the juices in, then reduce the heat a little and complete the cooking. Remove the steaks and keep them warm. To make the sauce, remove the pan from the heat and let it cool a little, add the wine and egg yolks, whisk them together until they foam and thicken slightly; you should not cook them but there must be enough heat to allow them to thicken. Take the pan off the heat and whisk in the melted butter to form a thick liaison.

Roll the wild garlic leaves up together like a cigar, then shred them along the lengths to give a very fine cut; mix them into the sauce and serve with the steaks. You can adjust the seasoning of the sauce and add lemon juice if you want a sharper taste.

Stovies

The Auld Alliance comes in here: the word 'stovie' comes from the French 'étuve' which means to stew in its own juices. I have eaten many stovies, some excellent and some not so, and prepared in all sorts of ways. Stovies I had as a child were always made with sliced potatoes and dripping not, as I have tasted, with over-boiled potatoes and tinned corned beef!

Traditionally served with cold meats or on its own as a supper dish.

Melt the dripping in a large pan, strew in the onion and cook gently to soften. Add the lamb and then season. Finally put in the potatoes in an even layer and cover them with the stock. Bake in a medium oven, 190°C/375°F/Gas 5 until the liquid is absorbed and the edges of the potato are browned, this takes about 50 minutes.

INGREDIENTS

125g / 4oz cold cooked lamb, diced

750g / 1½lb potatoes, evenly sliced

1 large onion, peeled and sliced

1 tbsp dripping

300ml / 10fl oz beef stock

salt and pepper

SERVES 4

Lamb Hot Pot

A turn-of-the-nineteenth-century dish, which no doubt developed over the years before that.

Trim the chops of all fat and bone. Slice the kidneys in half horizontally, then remove the fat and core. Put three chops on the base of a deep casserole and season well. Add a layer of kidney, then a layer of onion and finally a layer of potato. Repeat, seasoning each layer, and finishing with a layer of potatoes.

Heat the stock and pour it over the top, barely covering the ingredients, cover and cook in a moderate oven, 180°C/350°F/Gas 4 for about 1½ to 2 hours. Remove the lid for the last 30 minutes to brown the top.

INGREDIENTS

6 lean lamb chops

6 lambs' kidneys, skinned

500g / 1lb potatoes, sliced

1 medium onion, peeled and sliced

salt and pepper

600ml / 1 pint brown stock (see p136)

SERVES 4

Boiled Gigot of Lamb with Capers

Traditionally mutton would have been boiled in water with vegetables, and would have been real mutton, full of flavour but needing long cooking. It is hard to get hold of mutton nowadays, since lamb provides a quicker return on a farmer's investment; it should really be treated as different meat. Lamb at the end of the season, just before the new lamb comes in, can be cooked in this method, or true mutton if you can get it. Do not use young lamb, since that is far better cooked pink and this dish needs to be well cooked.

The milk is important for poaching since it helps the colour of the meat, quite apart from the flavour.

Trim the joint of any fat, place it in a deep saucepan and pour on the milk; I find adding a little water makes the final sauce a little less rich. Put in the onions, carrots, herbs, black peppercorns and salt. Cover and bring to the boil, simmer gently for 2 to 3 hours or until the meat is cooked through. There should be no blood in the juices when you push a skewer into the middle of it. Take the meat out and keep it hot. Strain the stock and let it simmer for 10 minutes then reserve 900ml (1½ pints) for the sauce.

In another pan melt the butter and add the flour, stir for a few moments, add the warm milk stock, stirring all the time, no lumps should appear if the milk is hot; if lumps do appear just whisk or beat them out. Add the capers and a little juice.

To serve, slice the lamb quite thickly, coat it with the sauce and sprinkle on some fresh chopped parsley.

INGREDIENTS

1 leg of mutton, boned and rolled

2 large onions, each peeled and stuck with 2 cloves

2 carrots, peeled and roughly chopped

1 sprig rosemary

1 bay leaf

6 black peppercorns

1 sprig each of fresh parsley and thyme

milk to cover

salt

2 tbsp fresh parsley, chopped

Caper sauce

2 tbsp plain flour

2 tbsp butter

3 tbsp capers and a little juice

900ml / 1½ pints cooking juices

salt and pepper

SERVES 10

Devilled Lambs' Kidneys

INGREDIENTS

12 lambs' kidneys

3 tbsp vegetable oil

1 tbsp Worcester sauce

1 tbsp mushroom ketchup

pinch cayenne

175g / 6oz butter

2 tsp each of dry mustard
   powder and French mustard

SERVES 4

This recipe probably came out of the need to disguise meat which was past its best, or 'high', and has become something of a Scottish favourite. The word 'devilled' simply refers to the fiery combination from which the sauce is normally made.

In the 1950s, one hotel used to buy chickens from such a distance that by the time they got to the hotel, they were so high that the only way to cook them was to curry them; the hotel got quite a reputation for its superb chicken curry!

Skin the kidneys and trim off the fat, slice them in half horizontally and cut out the core. Heat the oil in a frying pan and cook the kidneys quickly on both sides. Leave them a little pink in the middle. Mix together all the other ingredients in a bowl. Pour off the excess fat from the pan, spread the devilling mixture over the kidneys until well combined and the butter melts. Serve with rice.

Lambs' Liver
with lemon and honey

INGREDIENTS

lambs' liver (allow just over
   175g / 6oz per person)

1 tbsp plain flour

salt and pepper

1 tsp blossom or heather
   honey

juice of ½ lemon

1 tbsp vegetable oil

50g / 2oz butter

SERVES 4

This is my mum's dish; what more can I say – I love it.

Cut the liver into strips. Season the flour with salt and pepper. Coat the liver in the flour, shaking off any excess. Heat a pan, add a little oil and butter and cook the liver very quickly to just colour it, then remove it from the pan. Reduce the heat, add the honey and lemon and bring to the boil, then return the liver to the pan just to coat it with the sauce. Serve immediately. Good with pilaff rice (see Kedgeree, p61) and a crisp salad.

Saddle of Lamb with Herb Stuffing

Place the saddle, fat-side down, and trim away the fat but do not cut through the skin; leave the side 'flaps' intact but fat free. You should have the saddle, 2 fillets, trimmings and bones.

The stock: Roast the bones in a hot oven, 200°C/400°F/Gas 6 until they are brown. Put the lamb trimmings into a pan and cook to release the fat; add the chopped onion and carrot; when they are all lightly browned add the lamb bones from the oven, then add the red wine and top up with water to cover. Bring to the boil and as it comes to the boil turn the heat down to a simmer; skim off the froth and fat which come to the surface. Add the herbs, simmer for 1 hour. Strain and set aside.

The stuffing: In a frying pan sweat the shallot in a little olive oil until soft, add the breadcrumbs; remove from the heat. Mix in the tarragon and the beaten egg to bind, season. Turn the saddle onto its flesh side and make slashes across the fat diagonally first one way then the other, do not pierce right through to the meat, this helps to release the fat when it cooks. Turn it back onto the skin side, season with salt and pepper and push the stuffing into the space left by the bone. Press the 2 fillets on top and fold the flaps over. If they overlap cut a little off each one so they just meet in the middle. Tie it up with twine, securing well all the way down.

To cook: Keep the lamb at room temperature for at least 1 hour before cooking. Rub over the skin with salt and butter. Roast in a hot oven, 230°C/450°F/Gas 8 for 20 minutes, to really brown the fat. Turn the heat down to 200°C/400°F/Gas 6 and cook for another 15 minutes. Leave to rest in a warm place for at least 20 minutes before carving.

Sprinkle the flour into the roasting tray and stir around over a high heat to catch the juices in the tray. Pour on the previously prepared stock and scrape up all the juices, add the rowanberry jelly and simmer until it melts. Strain into a clean pan and simmer until a light coating texture is achieved. You may need to skim off a little fat. To serve remove the string from the lamb and carve it into thick slices. Serve the sauce separately.

INGREDIENTS

1kg / 2lb saddle of lamb. Ask your butcher to remove the membrane from the saddle, remove the fillets, take the bone out and give you everything

1 tbsp olive oil

2 shallots, peeled and chopped

50g / 2oz white breadcrumbs

1 tbsp fresh tarragon, chopped

1 egg, beaten

salt and pepper

a little butter for roasting

Sauce
Part one

lamb bones, chopped up

1/2 onion, peeled and chopped

1 small carrot, peeled and chopped

150ml / 5fl oz red wine

water

1 sprig thyme

1 bay leaf

Part two

1 tbsp plain flour

1 tbsp rowanberry jelly (see p141)

SERVES 6

Braised Lamb Shanks with Butter Beans

INGREDIENTS

4 lamb shanks

2 tbsp olive oil

1 large onion, peeled and diced

1 large carrot, peeled and diced

1 large leek, peeled and diced

3 cloves garlic, crushed with salt

350g / 12oz butter beans

2 x 350g / 12oz cans chopped tomatoes

1 tbsp tomato purée

1 bay leaf

SERVES 4

I love lamb shanks and I don't believe that enough is made of them. They are so full of flavour and although you do not have to be too precise about cooking times, they need to be well cooked so that the meat falls off the bone. This dish, whilst not very traditional, makes use of the long slow 'all in the pot' cooking, and is perfect for a cold, dreich night. It is really best made a day in advance and reheated, allowing all the flavours to intermingle. You need to soak the beans overnight too.

Peel and cut the onion, carrot and leek into 6mm (¹/₄in) dice. Wash the beans in cold water and soak them overnight. The next day put them into a pan of water and bring to the boil, simmer gently for 30 minutes. Drain and put aside. Turn on the oven to 230°C/450°F/Gas 8. Season the lamb shanks and smother them in the olive oil, roast in the hot oven for about 10 minutes until well coloured. Turn the oven down to 190°C/375°F/Gas 5 and continue to cook for about 2 hours. Thirty minutes before the end add the diced vegetables, stir them in to collect some of the juices.

After the 2 hours bring the pan to the stove top, remove the lamb shanks and set them aside. Add the garlic to the pan and stir in, then add the drained butter beans, the tomatoes, with about 2 cans full of water (use the cans the tomatoes came in), the tomato purée and bay leaf. Bring to the boil and then return the lamb to the pan. Make sure the lamb is well covered by the bean mixture, add more water if necessary. Cook for another 30 minutes in the oven. The lamb should be falling off the bone and the beans soft with a little bite to them.

Braised Lamb Shanks with Butter Beans

INGREDIENTS

12 lamb cutlets

250g / 8oz pearl barley

*750ml / 1¼ pints chicken
stock*

75g / 3oz butter

*1 onion, peeled and finely
chopped*

*50g / 2oz Strathkinness
cheese*

olive oil

SERVES 4

Grilled Lamb
Cutlets with Barley Risotto

Barley Risotto

In a saucepan, bring the stock to the boil. Melt the butter in a heavy-based pan, add the chopped onion and sweat to soften: add the barley, stir to coat well, then add about one third of the stock. Bring it to the boil, stirring all the time over a gentle heat until the liquid is absorbed into the barley. Add more of the stock and continue to stir as the liquid is absorbed. Finally add the rest of the stock, stirring all the time. You will create a thick creamy mixture, and the barley will still have a little 'bite' to it.

Grate the cheese. When the barley has absorbed all the stock stir in the cheese, season and serve with a splash of olive oil.

This risotto can be served as a first course, but if you add lamb cutlets you get a sort of variation on hot pot.

Lamb Cutlets

It is best to use a cast-iron, ribbed grill or if cooking on an Aga use their ribbed griddle pan. Brush the lamb with olive oil and season with salt and pepper. Get the pan very hot, then char the lamb quickly, for perhaps 2 minutes, then rotate a quarter turn to get the criss-cross ribbed marks, then turn over for another 2 minutes. Sear briefly on the skin side to cook the fat properly but leave the meat pink.

Serve the lamb simply on a mound of risotto.

Haggis

Perhaps the one food which represents Scotland and the Scots most accurately. Well-known internationally far beyond its worth, mainly due to Robbie Burns's poem, the haggis is also an object of fun, with stories put about that it is a little animal, with two legs on one side longer than the other two, so that it can run round the hill and keep level; the way to catch it is therefore to run round the other way and have a colleague at the bottom of the hill to catch the poor beast as it topples over and rolls down! Visitors from all over the world always ask, 'What is actually in it?', ready to be horrified by the catalogue of unmentionable things they expect you to tell them is in it. Usually, of course, they say, 'Oh, is that it, we have something like that at home'!

The thriftiness of the Scot is there also, nothing is wasted. The sheep's pluck or stomach is cleaned and soaked in brine, then the heart, liver and lights (or lungs) are minced together with oatmeal, onion and seasoning. The pluck is stuffed and the whole thing is boiled for about 3 hours in stock. Delicious, but no more so than any other of the many puddings and pies produced in Scotland such as black pudding, Forfar Bridies or Scotch Pies.

I would advise you not to make your own, but to buy somebody else's instead; most local butchers make them so keep them in business or order from MacSween of Edinburgh, who make superb haggis, which they will send to you (see p157).

Serving a haggis is full of pitfalls as to what you should and should not do and as to what does and does not go. For me the best way is with mashed potato, moistened with milk and butter. The other accompaniment is generally 'bashed neeps' which are swedes (yellow turnips) mashed like potato and seasoned with butter, but not too much liquid otherwise it becomes too sloppy.

INGREDIENTS
1kg / 2lb haggis
1.25kg / 2½lb potatoes
750g / 1½lb yellow turnips,
* or swedes*

SERVES 4

Chicken in the Pot

There is no doubt that this is a traditional way of cooking, like the French 'pot au feu', a dish in which everything is cooked in the same pot, with items being added at different stages depending how long they take to cook. There would have been a tradition for this in Scotland also.

Take the onion, 1 carrot, 1 stick of celery and any trimmings, 1 leek and the green tops of the others. Put these in a pan with the chicken, peppercorns, bay leaf, thyme and parsley stalks. Cover with water and bring to the boil. Immediately it boils turn the heat down to a simmer and, using a ladle, skim off the fat and froth. You will need to do this from time to time. If the bird gets uncovered at any time, top it up with water. Cook for about 2 hours, until the chicken is tender but not quite falling off the bone.

Prepare the other vegetables in order of cooking speed – potatoes first then carrots, shallots, leek, celery and cabbage.

Remove the chicken from the pan and keep it warm. Strain the stock into a clean pot and bring it back to a simmer, skim again getting as much of the fat off as possible. Next add the vegetables, first the potatoes, then after a few minutes add the carrots, bring the liquid back to the boil and add the rest in succession, allowing the stock to return to the boil each time. When everything is in and the cabbage has had about 2 minutes in the water, remove all the vegetables with a slotted spoon.

In another pan, melt the butter and stir in the flour, slowly pour on the boiling stock stirring all the time until you have put in about 900ml (1^1/$_2$ pints), let the sauce simmer for 10 minutes to reduce to about 600ml (1 pint).

You can either serve the whole chicken with the vegetables scattered in a colourful array all around, or joint the chicken and serve it in large soup bowls. Check the sauce for seasoning, add the parsley and pour over the dish.

INGREDIENTS

1 boiling fowl

1 onion, peeled and studded
  with 4 cloves

8 small potatoes, left whole

8 shallots, peeled

3 medium carrots, peeled and
  sliced at an angle

3 sticks of celery, trimmed
  and sliced at an angle

3 small leeks, trimmed and
  washed

1 small cabbage, cut in
  quarters

1 bay leaf

water

6 black peppercorns

1 sprig thyme

3 parsley stalks

2 tbsp butter

2 tbsp plain flour

3 tbsp fresh parsley, chopped

SERVES 4-6

Stoved Chicken

Based around the stovie idea, (stovie is from the French *étuve*, which means to stew in its juices) this is a simple all-in-one type stew.

Dry the chicken joints on kitchen paper, then brown the pieces in half the butter, and set them aside. Sweat the onions until they colour slightly and soften. Grease the inside of a casserole dish, then put a layer of potato slices on the bottom, then a layer of onion, season with salt and pepper and dot with butter. Next put in a layer of chicken and season. Continue with the layers, finishing with a layer of potatoes at the top and a final dot with butter. Pour three-quarters of the stock over and cover. Cook in a low oven, 140°C/275°F/Gas 1 for at least 2 hours. If the stock seems to be drying out add the rest. When cooked, sprinkle with the chopped parsley.

INGREDIENTS

1 chicken jointed into 8
  pieces, skin removed
125g / 4oz butter
1¼kg / 2½lb potatoes, sliced
2 large onions, peeled and
  sliced
salt and pepper
600-900ml / 1-1½ pints
  chicken stock
3 tbsp fresh parsley, chopped

SERVES 4

Smoored Chicken

This is a traditional method of cooking quickly; 'smoor' simply means to smother.

Put the grill on at least 10 minutes before you prepare this. Cut the chickens through the backbone, using a pair of heavy kitchen scissors. Wipe the chicken and then dry it with kitchen paper. Place the chickens, skin-side down, on a grill rack, season and brush with melted butter. Grill until they begin to colour, this will take about 5 minutes. Turn them over and cook the other side for about 5 minutes, the fat should start to come out.

Mix the mustard with the milk and paint this over the skin and either continue to cook under the grill at a lower heat, or in the oven, 190°C/375°F/Gas 5, for about 15 to 20 minutes. When just ready, turn up the grill, sprinkle over the breadcrumbs, drizzle the rest of the butter over the top and brown lightly under the grill.

INGREDIENTS

2 young chickens, sometimes
  called 'poussin'
175g / 6oz butter, melted
salt and pepper
2 tsp mustard powder
3 tbsp milk
3 tbsp breadcrumbs

SERVES 4

Sauté of Chicken with a Piquant Sauce

Put the onions and about 15g ($^{1}/_{2}$oz) of butter with a little water into a heavy-based pan, cover and allow to cook gently for 20 minutes, without sticking, you will need to stir from time to time. If they do stick then add a little more water. Chop the tomatoes coarsely and add them to the pan with the garlic. Cook for another 5 minutes, then remove from the heat and leave in a warm place with the lid still on.

In a different pan, brown the pieces of chicken in another 15g ($^{1}/_{2}$oz) of butter, then put them on top of the tomato and onion mixture in the other pan, and allow to stew gently over a low heat, this takes about 15 minutes. Add the wine vinegar to the pan in which the chicken browned and over a high heat reduce to a syrup, then add the wine and reduce to about 150ml (5fl oz) of liquid.

To assemble
Place the cooked chicken on a dish and keep it warm; pour the tomato mixture on to the wine mixture and mix well, bring to the boil and strain through a fine sieve. Add the cream and any juices which have come from the chicken, season and serve over the chicken.

INGREDIENTS
1 chicken divided into 8 pieces
500g / 1lb red onions, peeled and sliced in thin rounds
50g / 2oz butter
2 cloves garlic, peeled and crushed
2 or 3 very ripe tomatoes
300ml / 10fl oz white wine vinegar
300ml / 10fl oz red wine
150ml / 5fl oz double cream
salt and pepper

SERVES 4

INGREDIENTS

1 chicken, approx. 1.5-2kg
  (3-4lb) or 8 chicken joints
175g / 7oz smoked streaky
  bacon
3 tbsp vegetable oil
25g / 1oz butter
black pepper
cocktail sticks

Marinade
1 litre / 1¾ pints red wine
2 medium carrots, peeled and
  roughly chopped
1 small onion, peeled and
  roughly chopped
1 bay leaf
1 sprig thyme
1 clove garlic, crushed

Sauce
1 tbsp plain flour
1 litre / 1¾ pints chicken
  stock (see p136)
5 tbsp double cream
1 tbsp blackcurrant cordial
salt and pepper

SERVES 4

Chicken with Red Wine & Smoked Bacon

This recipe is particularly good with a free-range bird because the almost gamey flavour marries well with the wine, the smoke and cordial. It also goes well with a cheap chicken which provides texture for all the above flavours! You will need to marinade it a day in advance.

To prepare and marinade the chicken
Cut the chicken into 8 pieces; legs in two, 2 winglets and cut the breast bone in half. Season with black pepper. Wrap the bacon around each piece and secure it with a cocktail stick. Put the chicken into a bowl and cover with the marinade ingredients. Leave in the marinade overnight.

To cook
Remove the chicken from the marinade, drain it, and dry on kitchen paper. Reserve the marinade liquid. Heat the oil in a frying pan and brown the chicken pieces all over. Put the butter in a casserole and add the drained vegetables from the marinade; cook them on the top of the stove for a couple of minutes, then add the flour and stir around to coat the vegetables. Cook for another 4 minutes, then add the pieces of chicken.

Drain off the fat from the pan the chicken was browned in, and pour the marinade liquid into the pan, bring to the boil, scraping up the juices from the bottom of the pan. Add the thyme, garlic and bay leaf. Pour the whole lot over the chicken and stir to mix in with the flour-coated vegetables. Add the stock and cook gently for about 20 minutes.

Remove the chicken and when it is cool enough to handle, pull out the cocktail sticks; keep the chicken warm. Simmer the stock and reduce it by half, this will take about 15 minutes. Stir in the cream and blackcurrant, and then strain it. Check for seasoning and serve over the chicken.

Chicken with Red Wine & Smoked Bacon

INGREDIENTS

1 roasting chicken, approx.
  2kg (4lb)

175g / 6oz butter

8 shallots, peeled

pinch of mace

2 whole cloves

6 black peppercorns

salt and pepper

600ml / 1 pint chicken stock
  (see p136)

1 chicken liver (optional)

1kg / 2lb fresh spinach

2 tbsp double cream

Stuffing

50g / 2oz fresh breadcrumbs

1 small shallot, peeled and
  chopped

1 tsp fresh tarragon, chopped

1 tsp fresh parsley, chopped

3 tbsp milk

salt and pepper

SERVES 4

Chicken Howtowdie

This is a magnificent dish with wonderful flavours. I have taken some liberties; I prefer not to put stuffing in the cavity of a chicken, but rather like the stuffing under the skin. I also make use of a liquidiser for the sauce since this gives a really smooth finish, which the original recipe cannot achieve. I hope the purists forgive me!

Mix together all the ingredients for the stuffing and using your fingers carefully lift the skin of the chicken away from the flesh and press the stuffing under the skin as far up as you can, covering the legs and breast.

Heat a large casserole which will hold the chicken with the lid on, add 75g (3oz) butter, when it foams brown the chicken all over, remove it and then brown the shallots. Put the chicken back into the casserole with the shallots around it and add the stock and spices. Cover and cook in a medium oven, 180°C/350°F/Gas 4 for about 1-1$\frac{1}{2}$ hours.

Wash the spinach and blanch it by putting it in boiling water for 2 minutes, then removing it and putting it into cold water to refresh it and halt the cooking process.

When the chicken is cooked, remove it from the dish and keep it warm. Drain the stock and let it cool a little. Take a little of the stock from the casserole and liquidise it with 15g (1oz) butter, the cream and the chicken livers. Return this to the rest of the stock, check for seasoning; do not let it boil. Take the drained spinach, squeeze out the excess water, put it in a pan and cook it quickly in the rest of the butter with lots of salt and pepper.

Serve on a large platter with the chicken in the middle, the spinach round the outside and the sauce poured over the top of the bird, but not on the spinach.

Scotch Eggs

Boil 8 of the eggs for 10 minutes then remove and cool in cold water. When cold shell them.

Beat 1 of the other 2 eggs with the tablespoon of cold water. Season the sausagemeat with the mace, salt and pepper. Dip a hard-boiled egg into the beaten egg and then cover it all over with sausagemeat, using your hands to press it on firmly. Repeat with the rest of the eggs. Beat the last raw egg on its own and roll the sausagemeat-covered eggs in it, and then coat them in the breadcrumbs. Deep fry the eggs in hot oil until golden brown, then drain well. The eggs can be served hot or cold.

INGREDIENTS

10 eggs

1 tbsp cold water

750g / 1½lb pork
  sausagemeat

pinch mace

salt and pepper

125g / 4oz breadcrumbs

cooking oil for deep frying

SERVES 4

Marinaded Pork Chops

Whilst there is no real tradition for pork in Scotland, it is a much underrated meat, and has much to offer in the wide variety of ways in which it can be cooked. It produces the most delicious gravy, it is essential in most terrines and on a summer evening what could be nicer than a pork chop on the barbecue!

Whisk together the oil and wine, add the remaining ingredients and pour over the pork chops, making sure that the meat is covered. Marinade the pork for a few hours before char grilling. They will roast very successfully also.

INGREDIENTS

4 pork chops

Marinade

150ml / 5 fl oz olive oil

150ml / 5 fl oz red wine

1 tbsp tomato purée

1 tbsp runny honey

1 tbsp wholegrain mustard

30ml / 1fl oz wine vinegar

1 clove garlic, crushed

SERVES 4

INGREDIENTS

500g / 1lb lean pork, diced

2 medium onions, peeled and
  chopped

1 clove garlic, crushed

2 tbsp olive oil

3 tbsp plain flour, seasoned
  with salt and pepper

approx. 300ml / 10fl oz
  Heather ale or dry cider

2 tbsp fresh chopped herbs,
  such as coriander, parsley,
  chervil, tarragon

SERVES 4

Casserole of Pork with Fresh Herbs & Heather Ale

A very simple dish using prime lean pork with a Scottish ale. Heather ale is made from heather flowers and has been produced in Scotland since the Dark Ages. Recently the tradition of brewing this ale has been revived. If you cannot find it then use dry cider instead.

Dry the pork with kitchen paper and then coat it in the seasoned flour, shaking off any excess flour. Put it on a plate. Heat the olive oil in a heavy-based frying pan, and brown the pork in small batches so that it does not stick; it is important to keep the temperature high, to prevent the pork from exuding its moisture.

Once all the meat has been browned put it into a casserole dish. Add the onion to the frying pan, let it soften and brown lightly, add to the pork, pour in a little water to just absorb the juices and pour over the pork. Pour in the Heather ale, or cider, and bring to the boil. Cover the pan and allow the pork to simmer for about $1^{1}/_{4}$ hours or until tender, or put it into a medium oven, 180°C/350°F/Gas 4. Five minutes before removing from the heat add the chopped herbs. If the casserole is too watery, allow to simmer on the stove top without the lid for a few minutes until it thickens slightly. Serve with mashed potatoes.

Puddings

Tayberry Tart (p114)

INGREDIENTS

600ml / 1 pint double cream

75g / 3oz pinhead oatmeal, toasted

6 tbsp whisky

3 tbsp Scottish honey

500g / 1lb raspberries

SERVES 4

INGREDIENTS

350g / 12 oz greengages or other fruit

50g / 2oz caster sugar

350g / 12oz shortcrust pastry

1 egg, beaten with 1 tbsp milk.

SERVES 4-6

Cranachan

The classic Scottish pudding, good anyway but with really rich double cream, malt whisky, heather honey and Mr Rodger's oatmeal from Aberfeldy Watermill, it's something else!

Put the oatmeal onto a metal tray under a hot grill, toast for 3 to 5 minutes. Take care that it does not burn. Leave to cool.

Lightly whip the cream and fold in the whisky and honey, then fold in the oatmeal and berries. Pour into tall glasses, and chill for at least 1 hour before serving, or overnight.

Greengage Frushie

'Frushie' is an old Scottish word meaning brittle or crumbly and probably refers here to the texture of the pastry used in this Victorian tart. It is traditional to the west of Scotland and many different fruits can be used, gooseberries or apples being the most common.

Line a 20cm (8in) flan dish with shortcrust pastry. Arrange the stoned fruit on top with sugar to taste, then put strips of pastry in a lattice shape, over the top. Brush the pastry with milk and beaten egg and bake in a moderate oven, 200°C/400°F/Gas 6 for 30 to 40 minutes.

Serve warm or cold, with cream.

Clootie Dumpling

This is the one that everyone remembers their granny making, and has taken on the mantle of porridge in that everyone has their own way of doing it. In Scotland people cannot always recognise the regional recipes, but there are certainly regional methods! I bow at this point not to my granny, who certainly showed me how to use a 'girdle', but to Theodora Fitzgibbon.

The name is simply reflective of the fact that the pudding is traditionally cooked in a cloth or 'cloot', although you can also make it in a pudding basin.

Using your fingertips, rub the fat into the flour, and add the oatmeal, sugar, baking powder, fruit and spices. Mix in well then add the syrup and eggs. Stir all together, adding enough milk to form a firm batter.

If you are using a pudding cloth, it should be either a linen or cotton cloth, about 55cm square (8$\frac{1}{2}$ in sq.) Plunge it first into boiling water, remove it carefully then lay it out and sprinkle flour over it. Place the pudding mixture in the middle of the floured cloth and then tie it up leaving plenty of space for the pudding to expand.

Put an inverted plate or saucer at the bottom of a deep pan, put the dumpling in and cover it with boiling water, and cook for 2$\frac{1}{2}$ to 3 hours over a low heat.

If you are using a pudding basin, lightly grease the inside and put the mixture in allowing at least 2.5cm (1in) space at the top. Cover with greaseproof paper and tie down well. Either place in a bain marie with the water up to the rim and boil over a low heat for 2$\frac{1}{2}$ to 3 hours, or steam over a double boiler. Turn out onto a large warm plate. Serve in slices with hot jam and cream.

INGREDIENTS

125g / 4oz suet

250g / 8oz plain flour

125g / 4oz oatmeal

75g / 3oz sugar

1 tsp baking powder

*250g / 8oz mixed sultanas
and currants*

*1 tsp each of cinnamon
and ginger*

1 tbsp golden syrup

2 eggs, lightly beaten

3-4 tbsp milk

*1 tbsp flour for the cloot,
or cloth*

SERVES 4

Summer Pudding

One of my favourite puddings, ideal when there is a glut of summer fruits; once in a pudding they keep longer than if kept fresh. I find this recipe works best if strawberries comprise at least half of the total amount of fruit. It needs to refrigerate overnight.

Neatly line the base and sides of a 900ml (1^1/$_2$ pint) pudding basin with the bread. Wash and trim or stone the fruit, cutting the strawberries in half. Put the water and the sugar into a pan and bring to the boil. Add the fruit in order of speed of cooking, the slowest first and the quickest, raspberries, last. Cook briefly, ensuring that the fruit holds its shape. Drain off the syrup and reserve.

Spoon the fruit into the prepared bowl and spoon over a little of the syrup. Cover with more bread. Put a saucer on top and place a weight on top of it, to apply a little pressure, say 500g (1lb). Refrigerate overnight. Loosen it gently with a palette knife, turn out and pour the rest of the syrup over it. Cut into wedges and serve with lightly whipped double cream.

INGREDIENTS

slices of medium or thin
sliced crustless white bread
500g / 1lb fresh seasonal
fruit, eg. strawberries,
raspberries, cherries,
brambles
30ml / 1fl oz water
150g / 5oz caster sugar

SERVES 4-6

Summer Pudding

INGREDIENTS

250g / 8oz plain flour

150g / 5oz butter

50g / 2oz caster sugar

1 egg

INGREDIENTS

250g / 8oz sweet pastry

250g / 8oz dried prunes,
 softened and stoned

125ml / 4fl oz double cream

2 eggs

75g / 3oz caster sugar

50g / 2oz ground almonds

60ml / 2fl oz whisky

2 tbsp orange flower water

25g / 1oz butter

Sweet Pastry

This is a very useful recipe, and sweet pastry forms the basis of several fruit tarts in this book. The quantities of ingredients given here make enough pastry to line two 20cm (8in) flan dishes.

Cream the butter and sugar together in a blender or mixer. Add the flour and continue to beat until just combined. Add the egg and mix until well combined. Leave in a cool place for 1 hour before use.

Prune & Whisky Tart

A Scottish version of a classic French tart.

Line a 20cm (8in) flan tin with the pastry. Prick the base and leave in a cool place for 1 hour before use.

Put the cream, eggs, sugar, ground almonds and orange flower water in a large bowl and whisk together. Melt the butter and pour it into the egg mixture, whisking it thoroughly.

Arrange the prunes in the bottom of the flan dish and pour the mixture over the top. Bake in the oven at 200°C/400°F/Gas 6 for 25 minutes. When cooked, sprinkle the tart with the whisky, and serve warm.

Rhubarb Tarts

Wash the rhubarb, trim off the edges and cut it down the middle, then cut into pieces about 1cm ($^1/_2$in) in length. Mix with just enough caster sugar to coat and leave for about 30 minutes, this brings out the moisture.

Roll out the pastry, and use a side plate to cut out a disk of puff pastry, about 3mm ($^1/_8$in) thick. Then use a saucer to mark a border about 3mm ($^1/_8$in) in from the edge, but do not cut through the pastry. Cut as many disks as there are people you want to feed.

When ready to cook put a baking sheet in the oven to heat. Spread the rhubarb over the pastry disks to cover, do not overlap the border.

Slide the pastry disks onto the heated baking sheet and cook for 15 minutes in a hot oven, 220°C/425°F/Gas 7. When cooked the edges should be lightly browned; dust lightly with icing sugar, and serve on individual plates with whipped cream.

INGREDIENTS

250g / 8oz puff pastry

125g / 4oz caster sugar

50g / 2oz icing sugar

625g / 1$^1/_4$lb rhubarb

SERVES 4

Caramelised Apple Tart

INGREDIENTS

7 large eating apples such as
  James Grieve or
  Rev. Wilkes
210g / 7oz caster sugar
210g / 7oz butter
250g / 8oz sweet pastry (see
  p110)
1 egg, beaten

SERVES 4

This is one of those recipes you have to do once, to find out your own measurements, since every frying pan is different. Quantities given here are for a 26cm (10in) diameter tart.

Use a shallow pan which will fit into the oven, about 26cm (10in) in diameter.

On the stove top add the sugar and butter to the pan and allow to caramelise over a low heat, gently stirring all the time. It takes about 10 minutes.

Meanwhile cut the apples in half and then in quarters, peel and core them then cut in half again. When the butter and sugar are caramelised, place the apples carefully into the pan in a circular fan, until the pan is full. Take care not to burn your fingers. The pan should be full.

Lower the heat and cook gently for 5 minutes. Remove from heat. Roll out the pastry to a circle big enough to fit over the pan and spread it over, brush the top with eggwash. Put the pan into a hot oven, 200°C/400°F/Gas 6 and bake for about 30 minutes.

When cooked, remove from the oven and leave to rest for 10 minutes. To serve, gently reheat on the stove for a few minutes and then turn it out onto a warm plate. The pastry forms the base with the caramelised apples on top.

INGREDIENTS

250g / 8oz sweet pastry (see
  p110)

pastry cream (see p139)

approx. 125-175g / 4-6oz
  tayberries

icing sugar

SERVES 4

Tayberry Tart

It was a joy to return to Scotland after working abroad and in
the south, and to discover the tayberry. A cross between the
raspberry and the bramble, it is superb to cook with. If you
want to eat them raw, they must be very ripe, when they have
the most wonderful, perfumed flavour with an intense depth. In
cooking they are first class, and don't need to be so ripe. This
recipe uses pastry cream, the rich sweetish 'custard' which
provides the foil to the slightly sharp tayberry.

Line a 20cm (8in) flan case with the pastry and leave it in a cool
place for 1 hour, then bake the flan case blind in a hot oven,
200°C/400°F/Gas 6 for about 15 minutes. Leave to cool. Spread
enough pastry cream over the base of the flan to a depth of about
3mm (^{1}/$_8$in). Wipe the tayberries and push the stalk end gently
into the pastry cream. Start at the edge and in a circular motion
fill the whole tart. Just before serving dust with icing sugar.

INGREDIENTS

250g / 8oz sweet pastry
  (see p110)

350g / 12oz plums

90ml / 3fl oz double cream

2 large eggs

20g / ³/₄oz butter

50g / 2oz caster sugar

50g / 2oz ground almonds

SERVES 4

Plum Clafoutis

Plums have a short season and this is a good recipe for when
they are first on the scene, before you want to put them into
crumbles and chutneys. You can use other fruit in this recipe,
eg raspberries.

Line a 20cm (8in) flan case with the pastry, prick the base all over
with a fork and leave it to rest. Put the eggs, cream, sugar and
ground almonds into a bowl and whisk them together.

Melt the butter and pour into the mixture. Halve and stone the
plums and place them, cut-side down, in a circle on the pastry
until the whole base of the tart is covered. Pour the cream
mixture over the top. Bake in the oven at 200°C/400°F/Gas 6 for
25 minutes. Serve warm.

Plum Crumble

This is based on a traditional recipe which uses oatmeal as well as flour, which gives it a lovely nutty taste and texture. The oatmeal absorbs the plum juices to create a heavenly thick liquid sauce. You can use other fruits such as apples, brambles and even rhubarb.

Cook the fruit with the sugar, water and lemon juice until just softening. Put into a deep pie dish. Rub together the crumble ingredients, you should get the texture of breadcrumbs. Sprinkle evenly over the fruit and bake at 200°C/400°F/Gas 6 for 20 minutes or until the top is crunchy and brown.

INGREDIENTS

500g / 1lb stoned plums

50g / 2oz soft brown sugar

1 tbsp water

squeeze of lemon juice

50g / 2oz plain flour

25g / 1oz coarse oatmeal

50g / 2oz soft brown sugar

50g / 2oz butter, softened but not melted

SERVES 4

Bramble Fool

A celebration of summer fruits, intense, perfumed and luscious. Serve with shortbread fingers.

In a heavy-based pan cook the brambles with the sugar, covered, over a very low heat, no water is needed. Allow to cool and purée in a food processor, then push the purée through a fine sieve. The result is a thick, dark purée.

Combine 2 parts purée with 1 part pastry cream (see p139), then fold in 1 part whipped double cream. Pour into wine glasses and chill.

INGREDIENTS

500g / 1lb brambles

75g / 3oz soft brown sugar

whipped double cream

pastry cream (see p139)

SERVES 4

Drambuie Ice Cream

This is such a delicious ice cream, it is really more of a parfait. It makes an ideal accompaniment to soft fruit and warm puddings.

In a small saucepan add 6 tablespoons of water to the sugar and bring to the boil for a few seconds, then set aside.

Over a bain marie, whisk the egg yolks, when they are light in colour and texture add the hot sugar. Whisk the mixture until it forms a ribbon, then remove from the heat and continue to whisk until it is cool.

Add the liqueur and the lightly whipped cream. Freeze for 6 hours, or overnight.

INGREDIENTS

125g / 4oz caster sugar

6 tbsp water

6 egg yolks

210ml / 7fl oz double cream, lightly whipped

3 tbsp Drambuie

SERVES 4

Blaeberry Ice Cream

These beautifully flavoured berries are a hassle to pick but well worth the effort, even if they are rather small. The woods around us in Fife are awash with them and annual family trips are organised to collect them. They need little cooking.

Cook the fruit and brown sugar together over a low heat until cooked. This takes only a few minutes. Push through a fine sieve, leave to cool. In a small saucepan add 6 tablespoons of water to the caster sugar and bring to the boil for a few seconds, then set aside.

Over a bain marie, whisk the egg yolks, when they are light in colour and texture add the hot sugar. Whisk the mixture until it forms a ribbon, then remove from the heat and continue to whisk until it is cool.

Add the blaeberry purée and the lightly whipped cream. Freeze for 6 hours, or overnight.

INGREDIENTS

250g / 8oz blaeberries

50g / 2oz brown sugar

125g / 4oz caster sugar

6tbsp water

6 egg yolks

210ml / 7fl oz cream, lightly whipped

SERVES 4

Bramble Fool and Blaeberry Ice Cream

INGREDIENTS

Praline

125g / 4oz caster sugar

30ml / 1fl oz water

125g / 4oz hazelnuts, roughly
  chopped

Mousse

6 egg whites

275g / 9oz caster sugar

210ml / 7 fl oz double cream

300ml / 10fl oz single cream

SERVES 16

Iced Hazelnut Parfait

This will make enough to fill two loaf tins, one to use and one to keep, since this will keep in the freezer for several weeks. Don't be too horrified by the sugar and cream since there is enough to feed 16! Needs to freeze overnight.

Prepare the praline

Put the sugar and water into a heavy-based pan and bring to the boil. When the sugar begins to turn golden brown stir in the hazelnuts. Mix them around to coat with the caramel, then pour the mixture onto an oiled tray. Take great care as it is very hot.

Let it cool and then crush into small pieces using a small rolling pin or a pestle and mortar. The resulting mixture can be kept in an airtight jar for a week or more.

Mousse

Whisk the egg whites and sugar in a bowl over a pan of hot water until the sugar dissolves. Remove from heat and whisk until cold. An electric whisk or food processor saves the wrist! Mix the creams together and whisk until they thicken slightly. Fold the cream into the egg mixture and add the praline. Pour into a rectangular loaf tin lined with cling film and freeze overnight.

To demold

Warm the tin briefly by putting the base in hot water, this will soften the parfait slightly and it will then turn out onto a board. Peel off the cling film and either serve immediately or return to the freezer until needed.

To serve

Heat a knife in a jug of hot water, this will help it to slice through the parfait cleanly. Cut slices about 3mm ($^1/_8$in) thick and serve with raspberry sauce (see p139).

Rhubarb & Ginger Soufflé

Rhubarb and ginger is a wonderful combination, this light soufflé will really bring the flavours out.

Wash and trim the rhubarb and cut it into 1cm (¹/₂in) pieces. Stew the rhubarb and ginger in a pan with no water and a small amount of sugar, depending on the age of the fruit. Purée when cool.

Put the oven on to 200°C / 400°F / Gas 6.

Beat the rhubarb purée into the pastry cream and check for taste, add sugar or ground ginger depending on your preference. Prepare 4 ramekins: butter the inside and coat with caster sugar.

Whisk the egg whites in a grease-free bowl with a pinch of salt, until they peak, you should almost be able to turn the bowl upside down without them falling out, and fold about a third into the rhubarb mix. Return this to the bowl of egg whites and fold in gently with a plastic spatula. Pour carefully into the prepared ramekins and bake for about 15 minutes until risen and brown.

INGREDIENTS

250g / 8oz pastry cream
  (see p139)
approx. 250g / 8oz raw
  rhubarb to give 175g / 6oz
  when stewed
caster sugar
1cm / ¹/₂in piece root ginger,
  peeled and chopped
sugar or ground ginger to
  taste
4 egg whites
pinch salt

SERVES 4

Crème Brulée

This remarkable pudding dates back to Aberdeenshire of the 18th century, although it has been credited as having been invented by Cambridge University and by the French; I need say no more, except that it is delicious on its own or, as here, served with a little pot of hot stewed fruit (which incidentally is also delicious served over ice cream). It needs to chill overnight before serving.

Mix the egg yolks thoroughly with the sugar, then put the cream and the vanilla pod into a heavy-based pan. Bring to just below boiling point but do not boil, and add the vanilla essence if the pod is not available. Pour on to the egg yolks, stirring all the time until the mixture thickens, do not let it boil. Strain into a pie-dish and let it get cold, preferably overnight.

Get the grill very hot, then cover the surface of the cream evenly with the caster sugar, but do not make too thick a layer. Put at once under the grill and let the sugar melt and turn golden brown. Take from the heat and let it stand in a cold place for about 3 hours before serving.

INGREDIENTS

4 egg yolks

1 tbsp caster sugar

600ml / 1 pint double cream

1 split vanilla pod or a few
  drops of vanilla essence

approx. 50g / 2oz caster sugar

SERVES 4

Fruit Compôte

You can use your own combination of fruits, although I find that passion fruit adds a wonderful perfumed flavour. All the fruit must be ripe to get maximum juice and flavour.

Mix all the ingredients in a pan and stew gently over a low heat, until softened and combined; you should need no liquid since the sugar will bring the moisture out of the raspberries and brambles. Serve hot.

INGREDIENTS

1 passion fruit, halved and
  seeds removed

50g / 2oz raspberries

50g / 2oz brambles

1 ripe nectarine, cut into 8
  wedges

50g / 2oz brown sugar

SERVES 4

Crème Brulée and Fruit Compôte

Bread & Baking

INGREDIENTS

500g / 1lb strong flour

1/2 tbsp dried yeast

1 tbsp soft brown sugar

250g / 8oz butter

125g / 4oz lard

450ml / 15fl oz warm water

pinch salt

MAKES 16

Buttery Rowies

This is a traditional roll from Aberdeen and the best ones still come from there. Here is a traditional recipe.

Mix the yeast with the sugar and a little warm water to make a paste. Set aside. Mix the flour in a basin with the salt. When the yeast has bubbled up pour it into the flour with the rest of the water. Mix well to produce a dough and leave it to rise in a warm place.

Cream the butter and lard together and divide into three. The mixture should be soft enough to spread but not warm enough to melt.

When the dough has doubled in size, knock it back, this means knead it again until the dough is back to its original size, and then roll it out to a rectangle about 1cm ($^1/_2$in) thick. Spread a third of the butter mixture over two-thirds of the dough.

Fold the other third of dough over onto the butter, and the last third onto it, thus giving three layers. Roll this out back to the original size.

Leave to rest in a cool place for at least 40 minutes and repeat the above procedure, including leaving it to rest, twice more, to finish the butter mixture. Cut the dough into 16 squares. Shape into rough circles by folding the edges in all the way around.

Leave to rise, covered with a dry cloth, for 45 minutes. Bake in a hot oven, 200°C/400°F/Gas 6 for 15 minutes.

White Rolls

This is a very basic white loaf recipe which is good for rolls too. You can add things to it like sun-dried tomatoes, or chopped walnuts, and sprinkle things on top like poppy seeds, or sunflower seeds.

Put the flour into a large bowl with the salt and leave it in a warm place. Meanwhile put the yeast, sugar and about half the warm water into a jug. Mix to dissolve. Leave in a warm place, with a cloth over the top, until the yeast begins to froth; this takes about 10 minutes.

When the yeast is ready, pour it onto the flour and mix in. Knead by hand or using a mixer with a dough hook. The texture should be moist but should not stick to your hands.

Form it into a ball and cover the bowl. Leave it to double in size in a warm place. Knock it back, this means to knead again until the dough is back to its original size.

Divide the dough into 16, take each piece in your hand and form it into a ball, pulling the dough from the top to the bottom to give the top a smooth look. Place on lightly oiled oven trays, cover with a cloth and leave to rise again in a warm place, for about 30 minutes.

Bake in a hot oven, 200°C/400°F/Gas 6 for about 20 minutes, until brown.

INGREDIENTS

500g / 1lb strong white flour

2 tsp salt

275 ml / 10fl oz warm water

2 tsp dried yeast

2 tsp brown sugar

2 tbsp vegetable oil

MAKES 16

INGREDIENTS

1.5kg / 3lb wholemeal flour

3 tsp dried yeast

3 tsp brown sugar or honey

750ml / 1¼ pints warm water

2 tsp salt

MAKES 3 LOAVES

Brown Bread

This recipe is for a very basic wholemeal brown loaf, it is quite solid but full of flavour. If you prefer a lighter texture, use some ordinary brown flour mixed with the wholemeal. It is a good idea to have all the ingredients and utensils at room temperature before you start, this will help to speed up the process.

Put the flour into a large bowl with the salt and leave it in a warm place. Put the yeast, sugar or honey, and about 150ml (5fl oz) of the warm water into a jug. Mix to dissolve. Leave in a warm place, with a cloth over the top, until the yeast begins to froth, this will take about 10 minutes.

Prepare three bread tins by greasing them thoroughly. Keep warm. When the yeast is ready, pour it onto the flour and mix in; add the remaining warm water, mixing well and eventually kneading by hand or using a mixer with a dough hook. The texture should be moist but should not stick to your hands. Divide into three and press into the tins.

Cover with a cloth and put the tins in a warm place for the dough to rise. This will take anywhere between 20 minutes and 1½ hours, depending on how warm it is. The loaves should double in size. Bake in a hot oven, 200°C / 400°F / Gas 7 until brown, this will be after about 20 minutes.

Brown Bread, White Rolls (p125) and Oatcakes (p129)

INGREDIENTS

Case

250g / 8oz flour

125g / 4oz butter

½ tsp baking powder

cold water

Filling

1kg / 2lb raisins

1.5kg / 3lb currants

250g / 8oz almonds, chopped

350g / 12oz plain flour

250g / 8oz soft brown sugar

2 tsp allspice

1 tsp each of ginger,
  cinnamon, black pepper and
  baking powder

1 flat tsp cream of tartar

1 tbsp brandy

150ml / 5fl oz milk

1 egg, beaten

Black Bun

The traditional sweetmeat eaten at Hogmanay. It needs to mature for several weeks. It is different from fruit cakes in that it is baked in a pastry case.

Case

Rub the butter into the flour, add the baking powder and mix to a stiff dough with the water. On a floured board roll out the dough to a thin sheet. Grease a 20cm (8in) loaf tin and line the tin with the dough, keep enough aside for the top.

Filling

Mix all the ingredients together except the milk. Add enough milk to moisten the mixture. Put it into the prepared tin and put the remaining pastry on top using milk or egg wash to make it stick. Prick the top with a fork and brush with egg wash.

Bake in a cool oven, 110°C/225°F/Gas ¼ for about 3 hours. When cool, store in an airtight tin.

Oatcakes

Traditionally oatcakes are cooked on a girdle, but can be baked in the oven. The rolling and cutting out must be done quickly since if it cools the paste is not easily worked. Don't try to make large amounts of dough. To do larger quantities just repeat the process until you have made enough.

Mix the meal with the salt and bicarbonate. Pour in the melted fat and mix in. Add enough hot water to create a stiff paste. On a floured board roll out, either into a circle and cut it into quarters, or into a rectangle and cut it into triangles; place on the hot girdle, or in a medium oven, 190°C/375°F/Gas 5 until just browned at the edges.

INGREDIENTS

125g / 4oz medium and fine
* oatmeal, mixed*
2 tsp lard
pinch bicarbonate of soda
pinch salt
hot water to mix

MAKES ABOUT 16

Tablet

Nick Nairn from Aberfoyle gave me this recipe, I lost the original but hope I have remembered it well enough to make it like his.

Place all the ingredients in a large pan and bring to the boil. Reduce the heat. Allow to simmer gently for about 30 to 40 minutes, stirring from time to time. When it reaches a dark caramel colour, take the pan off the heat and whisk the mixture hard to cool and thicken, then pour it into a baking tray measuring 30 x 24cm (12 x 9^1/$_2$in).

Leave it to set for 10 minutes, then cut it into squares or shapes. Leave it to harden then remove from the tray.

INGREDIENTS

420ml / 14fl oz tin condensed
* milk*
1kg / 2lb granulated sugar
270g / 9 oz butter
600ml / 1 pint hot water

Scotch Pancakes

Mix the flour, salt and sugar together, add the beaten egg and then the milk to make a thick batter.

Heat a well-greased girdle or pan and drop one or two small spoonfuls of batter onto it. Cook on one side until brown, after a minute or two they will rise up and bubble a little; then turn them over and bake on the other side.

These simple little pancakes are delicious served still warm with jam and whipped cream or syrup. They do not keep!

INGREDIENTS
100g / 4oz self raising flour
pinch of salt
50g / 2oz caster sugar
1 egg
milk to mix

MAKES 12

Border Tart

This tart is very good hot with cream or custard, or cold, served at coffee time or with a cup of tea.

Mix the sugar and butter together until a paste is formed. Add the almonds, eggs and essence.

When mixed together add the currants and mix in well. Spread the mixture evenly into the pre-baked flan case.

Bake in the oven at 180°C/350°F/Gas 4 for about 20 minutes. Combine the icing sugar and lemon juice and brush it gently over the tart as it comes out of the oven.

INGREDIENTS
1 x 15cm (6in) sweet pastry
  base pre-baked blind
  (see pp110 and 154)
50g / 2oz ground almonds
50g / 2oz caster sugar
50g / 2oz butter
50g / 2oz currants
1 egg
few drops almond essence
juice of ½ lemon
2 tsp icing sugar

Shortbread

It's a brave person who reinvents the wheel. There must be as many recipes for shortbread as there are inches of rain on Fort William in a year. Some call for a small quantity of rice flour or Farola, but this traditional recipe uses all flour.

Cream the butter and sugar together, then combine with the sieved flours and salt, do this gently using your fingertips. Shape into 2 rounds with your hands; do not roll. Put onto a baking sheet. Pinch the edges with thumb and finger to give a clean finish. Prick the base all over with a fork. Bake in a low oven, 140°C/275°F/Gas 1 for about 1 hour. Leave to cool, cut into the required shape and turn onto a rack.

INGREDIENTS

500g / 1lb plain flour
500g / 1lb self raising flour
500g / 1lb butter
225g / 8oz caster sugar
½ tsp salt

MAKES ABOUT 16 PIECES

Dundee Cake

In advance, mix together the cherries, sultanas, currants and mixed peel. Put into a bowl, cover and place in a cool oven, 110°C/225°F/Gas ¼ for about 20 minutes until well heated through. This brings out the juices. Mix once during the process. Allow to cool before continuing.

Grease and line a 20cm (8in) cake tin. Cream together the butter and sugar, when the mixture turns white, add the eggs, one at a time, with a teaspoon of flour each time. Fold in the ground almonds and add the dried fruit, mixed peel, lemon rind and juice. Mix in the rest of the flour with the baking powder. Mix in the brandy. Pour into the prepared tin, cover with foil and bake in a low oven, 150°C/300°F/Gas 2 for about 2½ hours. Halfway through, remove the paper and spread the almonds on top. When cooked, brush with the milk and honey and return to the oven for another 5 minutes to give a glaze.

INGREDIENTS

175g / 6oz butter
175g / 6oz sugar
4 eggs
1 heaped tbsp ground
  almonds
250g / 8oz sultanas
250g / 8oz currants
75g / 3oz mixed peel, chopped
2 tbsp milk, boiled with
  1 tbsp honey
75g / 3oz halved glacé cherries
grated rind and juice of
  ½ lemon
250g / 8oz plain flour
1 tsp baking powder
1 tbsp brandy
25g / 1oz blanched split
  almonds

Border Tart (p131), Shortbread, Dundee Cake,
Buttery Rowies (p124) and Scotch Pancakes (p131)

Miscellany

A selection of fresh Scottish herbs

INGREDIENTS

Fish Stock

2kg / 4lb fish bones

1 onion, peeled and sliced

3 fresh parsley stalks

1 stick celery, chopped

1 medium carrot, peeled and
   chopped

3.5 litres / 6 pints water

5 peppercorns

1 bay leaf

Chicken Stock

2 chicken carcasses

1 medium carrot, peeled and
   sliced

1 onion, peeled and sliced

1 stick celery, chopped

3 fresh parsley stalks

1 sprig thyme and 1 bay leaf

water to cover

Brown Stock

2kg / 4lb bones, chicken or
   game carcasses

2 onions, peeled and chopped

1 large carrot, peeled and
   chopped

2 sticks celery, chopped

2.5 litres / 4 pints water

4 fresh parsley stalks

1 sprig thyme

1 tbsp oil

6 peppercorns

STOCK

There are lots of ways of making stock and all sorts of ingredients you can use, if you have a favourite method then by all means use it. If not here are three simple stocks which are suitable for use with the recipes in this book.

Fish Stock

Wash the bones thoroughly, in cold water. Put the onions on the bottom of a large pan then the bones. Add the water and bring slowly to the boil. As soon as it boils reduce the heat to a simmer and skim off the froth. Add the other vegetables and herbs and peppercorns. Allow to simmer gently for 20 to 30 minutes, no more or the stock will turn cloudy. It is also important not to let this stock boil rapidly as this too will cloud it. Allow to cool before straining through a sieve.

Chicken Stock

Wash the carcasses and put them into a large pan cover with water and bring to the boil. Remove the scum as it rises and when the stock boils reduce the heat and add the vegetables and herbs. Skim regularly as any froth or fat appears. Simmer for about 2 to 3 hours. Cool and strain.

Brown Stock

Roughly chop up the bones. Roast in a roasting tray in the oven, 200°C / 400°F / Gas 6 for about 30 minutes or until browned. While they are roasting, brown the vegetables in the oil in a large pan on the stove top. Add the bones and cover with water. Bring to the boil, skim off the scum and add the herbs and peppercorns. Simmer for 3 hours. Cool and strain.

Butter Sauce

This sauce is brilliant with poached fish and asparagus (see p54), but it is also very good made on its own. You can also flavour it by adding chopped herbs, such as chervil, tarragon or parsley, at the end.

Cut the butter into small chunks, keep cold. Put the wine vinegar, wine and onion into a small pan, preferably stainless steel, but not aluminium, the vinegar will react with it. Reduce the liquid over a gentle heat until there are about a couple of tablespoons left. Add the cream, when the liquid returns to the boil, take the pan away from the heat and whisk in the chunks of butter; if it cools too much then return the pan to the heat but do not allow the sauce to boil.

Do not stop whisking until the butter is completely incorporated into it, then add salt and pepper to taste. You can serve the sauce just like that with the tiny chunks of onion or strain it.

INGREDIENTS
75g / 3oz unsalted butter
3 tbsp white wine vinegar
5 tbsp dry white wine
1 tbsp double cream
2 tsp onion, chopped
salt and black pepper

Chervil Sauce

This is good served with salmon, asparagus or broccoli, especially if you use the water in which the salmon or vegetables have been cooked.

Put the wine and water into a saucepan, bring to the boil. Simmer to reduce the liquid by half, stirring all the time, then add the cream. Whisk in the butter away from the heat. Finally add the chopped chervil. The sauce should be of a texture to coat the back of the spoon. You may want to add a squeeze of lemon juice.

INGREDIENTS
2 tbsp fresh chervil, chopped
150ml / 5fl oz dry white wine
150ml / 5fl oz water
300ml / 10fl oz double cream
75g / 3oz butter
lemon juice (optional)

INGREDIENTS

6 tbsp dry white wine

6 tbsp white wine vinegar

3 shallots or ½ onion, peeled
*   and finely chopped*

250g / 8oz unsalted butter,
*   very cold and cut into*
*   chunks*

juice of 1 lemon

INGREDIENTS

1 onion, peeled and finely
*   chopped*

250g / 8oz wild mushrooms

50g / 2oz butter

25g / 1oz plain flour

150ml / 5fl oz double cream

salt and pepper

INGREDIENTS

2 tbsp white wine vinegar

2 tbsp olive oil

4 tbsp sunflower oil

3 tbsp wholegrain mustard

1 tbsp fresh dill, chopped

pinch of caster sugar

salt and pepper

Lemon Butter Sauce

A simple but effective sauce for shellfish; variations include using orange instead of lemon; adding fish stock when reducing gives a strong fish flavour. You can also use dry cider instead of wine vinegar. This powerful sauce is for serving with shellfish, not poured over it.

A stainless-steel pan with a handle is essential for this dish. If you have a gas ring make sure the flame does not come round the side of the pan, as it can burn easily. Combine the wine and vinegar in the pan with the shallots, simmer until the liquid has reduced to about 1 tablespoon. Away from the heat vigorously whisk in the butter, you will create a thick liaison. There are two important things to remember when you add the butter: don't allow the sauce to boil, if the butter is taking a long time to melt, put the pan back over a gentle heat to speed up the process, and you must whisk continuously until the butter is completely incorporated. Finally whisk in the lemon juice and check for seasoning. The sauce should be served warm.

Wild Mushroom Sauce

Melt the butter in a pan and add the onions, cook gently to soften. Wash and slice the mushrooms and add them to the pan. Cook gently for a few minutes and then add the flour. Stir gently without breaking up the mushrooms, add the cream and bring to the boil. Season.

Dill Mustard

In a processor combine the two oils, vinegar, sugar, whizz to emulsify; pour into a bowl and stir in the mustard and chopped dill and season.

Wild Garlic Sauce

This sauce is best made in a stainless-steel pan which will not react with the wine and lemon juice.

In the stainless steel pan, whisk the wine and egg yolks over a low heat, until they foam and thicken slightly; you should not cook them but there must be enough heat to allow them to thicken. Take the pan off the heat and whisk in the melted butter to form a thick liaison. Roll the wild garlic leaves up together like a cigar, then shred them along the lengths to give a very fine cut; mix them into the sauce. You can adjust the seasoning of the sauce and add lemon juice if you want a sharper taste.

INGREDIENTS
1 tbsp white wine
2 egg yolks
175g / 6oz melted butter
15 wild garlic leaves
lemon juice (optional)
salt and pepper

Pastry Cream

This is a very useful mixture, with a wide variety of uses. It is ideal for Bramble Fool (see p115) and also in fruit tarts and sweet soufflés (see pp114 and 119).

Heat the milk in a pan and add the vanilla. In a bowl whisk the egg yolks with the sugar until pale and creamy. Gradually stir in the flour and cornflour. Pour on the hot milk, whisking all the time. Put the mixture back into the pan and return it to the heat, stirring all the time until it thickens; it may go a little lumpy, but keep stirring and the lumps should cook out.

Remove from the heat and pour into a bowl. Cover with cling film or oiled greaseproof paper and leave to cool.

INGREDIENTS
425ml / 15fl oz milk
1 vanilla pod or few drops of
  vanilla essence
150g / 5oz caster sugar
5 egg yolks
2 level tsp plain flour
1 level tbsp cornflour

Raspberry Sauce

Purée the sugar and raspberries together and add lemon juice to taste, strain through a sieve.

INGREDIENTS
250g / 8oz raspberries
75g / 3oz caster sugar
squeeze of lemon juice

INGREDIENTS

1kg / 2lb Seville oranges

2 lemons

2.5 litres / 4 pints water

2kg / 4lb granulated sugar

Dundee Marmalade

The story goes that a merchant from Dundee bought a cheap shipment of oranges from Seville and when he discovered they were very bitter was all set to throw them away. His wife however turned them into a jam which sold very well! I like a bitter marmalade so you may prefer to use less sugar than specified in this traditional recipe, in which case cut out 500g (1lb).

Wash the fruit, leave it whole and place it in a large pan. Add the water, cover the pan and bring to the boil; simmer for about 1 hour until you can easily pierce the fruit. Carefully remove the fruit from the pan, retaining the liquid; when the fruit is cool enough to handle cut it into slices, whatever thickness you like; traditionally it was thick cut. It is easier if you whizz the fruit in a food processor for a minute, this gives small chunks of fruit which are easier to manage on toast.

Remove the pips and put them back into the water, simmer for another 10 minutes and strain into a preserving pan. Add the chopped fruit to the pan and the sugar, bring to the boil and simmer rapidly to setting point.

INGREDIENTS

2kg / 4lb tayberries

2kg /4lb granulated sugar

Tayberry Jam

This recipe produces a deeply coloured, intensely flavoured jam. If you prefer something less deeply scented, use a raspberry jam recipe and substitute tayberries for a quarter of the raspberries required. This will give the perfume without the incredible richness.

Wash and hull the fruit and put into a preserving pan, allow to soften in their own juices over a low heat, it will take about 15 minutes. Add the sugar and stir until dissolved. Bring to a rapid boil until setting point is reached.

Bramble Jam

The brambles should not be over ripe and should have a few red ones mixed in.

Wash the brambles and put them into a preserving pan with the lemon juice and water. Simmer gently until the fruit is cooked. Add the sugar, bring to the boil and boil rapidly to setting point.

INGREDIENTS
3kg / 6lb brambles
juice of 2 lemons
150ml / 5fl oz water
3kg / 6lb granulated sugar

Rowanberry Jelly

This is a truly Scottish condiment; made from the beautiful orange-red berries from the rowan, or mountain ash, it goes well with cold meats and is also excellent for cooking (see Roast Grouse with Rowanberries, p76).

The purists say this should be made with only rowanberries but I think the addition of apples makes this unique preserve less powerful. The pectin in the apples allows the jelly to set quicker than with pure rowanberries alone. Do try making it without apple, but be warned, it is strong!

Put the rowans, stalks and all, and the apples into a large saucepan, cover with water and boil for 40 minutes. Turn into a jelly bag or muslin and let it drip overnight into a bowl. Next day measure the amount of juice and allow 500g (1lb) sugar for every 600ml (1 pint) of juice. Bring the juice and sugar to the boil in a preserving pan or large saucepan, stirring to ensure that the sugar is dissolved. Continue boiling briskly until the temperature reaches 104°C/220°F. The best way to check is to test a few drops on a cold plate, when it forms a jelly it is ready.

INGREDIENTS
1.5kg / 3lb rowanberries
2 large cooking apples,
  chopped
water
granulated sugar

Potato Salad

We have such a lot of wonderful potato varieties in Scotland, usually of very high quality, often you can specify exactly what variety you want for a certain dish. This is a simple dish but it does need a semi-waxy potato which is not going break up at the edges. New season potatoes are not a problem since they often are waxy, for example, Maris Peer or Belle de Fontaney to name but two. Later in the year Kestrel are good, the small size is ideal and the pretty colour looks good too.

This salad goes well with smoked or pickled fish like gravadlax (p29) or marinaded mackerel (p34).

Cook the potatoes in salted water until just cooked, they should have a little bite to them. When they are nearly ready, simmer the chopped onion in a small pan with the wine vinegar until they reduce to about a tablespoon of liquid. Strain the potatoes through a colander and while still hot pour over the hot vinegar and onion mixture. The flavour is absorbed more readily when both are hot. Leave to cool and when cold moisten with a vinaigrette, add the parsley, and season with salt and pepper.

INGREDIENTS

1kg / 2lb small waxy potatoes washed and cut into 1cm (¹/₂in) pieces

150ml / 5fl oz white wine vinegar

1 small onion, peeled and chopped finely

2 tsp fresh parsley, chopped

1 tbsp vinaigrette

salt and pepper

Braised Red Cabbage

Great with game dishes, it also benefits from keeping.

Trim off and discard the outer leaves of the cabbage and cut it in quarters, remove the hard core or bone and shred the leaves finely. Soften the onions in the lard. Add the cabbage, stir to coat it in fat and heat it through. Raise the heat and add the vinegar. Steam for 2 minutes with a lid on. Lower the heat and stir in the redcurrant jelly and add the juniper and bay leaf. Continue to cook, covered, for about 50 minutes. When cooked, mix a little water with the cornflour and add this to the cabbage, stirring all the time, to thicken slightly.

INGREDIENTS

1 red cabbage, shredded

25g / 1oz lard

1 onion, peeled and sliced

2 tbsp redcurrant jelly

150ml / 5fl oz red wine vinegar

3 juniper berries

1 bay leaf

2 tsp cornflour

Potato Salad and Braised Red Cabbage

INGREDIENTS

500g / 1lb potato, boiled and
  mashed
500g / 1lb cabbage, shredded
125g / 4oz butter
4 spring onions, chopped
salt and pepper

INGREDIENTS

500g / 1lb potato, boiled
500g / 1lb yellow turnips, or
  swedes, boiled
50g / 2oz butter
pinch of nutmeg (optional)
2 tbsp chives, chopped
salt and pepper

Rumbledethumps

A Borders recipe, combining cabbage with potato, this is one of those dishes which can be varied in so many ways, and is often called 'bubble and squeak'.

Use a large frying pan which has a lid. Melt half the butter in the pan and add the cabbage, stir it gently to coat with the butter. When it is hot, cover, reduce the heat and cook very gently for 5 minutes. Remove the lid and raise the temperature to evaporate the liquid, mix in the mashed potato and spring onions, add the rest of the butter and mix well together and heat through. Season with salt and plenty of black pepper.

Clapshot

This is traditionally served with haggis, and is simply mashed potato and neeps (yellow turnip, also known as swede) mixed together. This is a very basic recipe, you can add warm milk to make a looser mixture and a little nutmeg is good too. If the dish is not for use with haggis, use less turnip for an unusual variation on mashed potato.

Boil the potatoes and turnips separately and let them dry in a colander in a warm place. Then mash them together with the butter, stir in the chives and season to taste.

Skirlie

Especially delicious with roast pork, also very good with roast game birds. It is much more interesting than breadcrumbs for absorbing meat juices.

Melt the butter in a pan and add the onion, fry gently to soften and colour lightly, add the oatmeal and stir in, season and allow to cook gently for 10 minutes.

INGREDIENTS

50g / 2oz butter
1 medium onion, peeled and
* finely chopped*
175g / 6oz medium oatmeal
salt and pepper

Porridge

What book on Scottish food would be complete without porridge? Nowadays it is easy to buy 'instant' rolled oats or even microwave porridge. For me the best porridge is made by cooking it overnight in an Aga, which gives a dreamy, creamy quality to the mix and doesn't leave a pan which is hard to clean! However, whatever your method, the quality of your meal is all important, new season's meal and as freshly ground as you can get. The Aberfeldy Watermill produces the best oatmeal I have yet found. Use a medium textured oatmeal.

Bring the water to the boil and slowly pour in the meal in a steady stream, while stirring all the time; when it returns to the boil reduce the heat, cover and simmer very gently for 15 minutes; add the salt, if you add it before this point it can harden the meal. Simmer again for another 10 minutes. Leave it to sit, covered, for 2 minutes, then serve. Tradition has it that it should be served in wooden bowls with a cup of milk; to eat it you dip your horn spoon first into the porridge, then into the milk; the only thing you add is salt! Honey is also delicious, or try a sprinkle of nutmeg or cinnamon, and OK, sugar if you must.

INGREDIENTS

125g / 4oz medium oatmeal
1.25 litre / 2 pints water
sea salt

SERVES 4

INGREDIENTS

1 small green Savoy cabbage,
  shredded

175g / 6oz smoked back
  bacon

3 tbsp olive oil

1 clove garlic, peeled and
  crushed

salt and pepper

Cabbage with Smoked Bacon

Cabbage doesn't always have a good press because it is often overcooked, but these two ingredients work so well together and are very simple to cook.

Remove and discard the tough outer leaves of the cabbage, cut it into quarters, cut out the centre core or bone and shred each quarter as finely as you can. Wash thoroughly and drain.

Cut the bacon into strips or lardons, fry quickly in a frying pan with the olive oil, add the cabbage and stir to coat in oil and heat through. Cover and cook for 3 to 4 minutes over a low heat. Remove the lid and raise the heat to evaporate the moisture. Season with salt and pepper.

INGREDIENTS

500g / 1lb carrots

1 tsp sea salt

50g / 2oz butter

1 tsp caraway seed

Carrots with Caraway

This is not a recipe to disguise poor quality carrots, you need good carrots, firm, full of flavour and colour.

Peel and cut the carrots into equal lengths, and cut them into batons. Plunge into boiling salted water for 4 minutes, remove and drain. Melt the butter in a pan, add the caraway and then the carrots, toss to mix through.

*Creamy Onion Tart (p38), Cabbage
with Smoked Bacon, Carrots with Caraway*

Reference

Rhubarb: widely grown and ever-popular

Seasonal Menus

One of the joys of exploring any regional cuisine is the chance to sample ingredients as they come into season. These four suggested menus draw on the finest combinations of Scottish fare.

Spring

This is the time of year when all the promise of the new season has just begun. Sea kale is perhaps over but the nettles are coming through, early young rhubarb, and the over-wintered leeks. I've chosen a menu which looks back to winter with a warming soup but on to the promise of summer with a crisp tart.

Cock a Leekie
Potted Crab
Pork Casserole with Fresh Herbs & Heather Ale
with mashed potato and spring greens
Rhubarb Tart

The soup can be a meal in itself , but if served sparingly, perhaps in small cups, it makes a delicious heart-warming first course.

Crab is just becoming good now and this simple dish makes an ideal middle course which can be prepared in advance and so causes little last-minute fuss.

The pork with herbs is perfect at this time of year and the fresh flavours signal the good times ahead.

To complete the meal the rhubarb tart really is a sign of the growth to come. Early rhubarb with its lovely young pink stalks makes a delicious pudding.

Summer

There is so much available at this time of year, it is impossible to choose: abundant salad items, young vegetables and of course the soft fruit; these are some of my favourite dishes.

Asparagus with Chervil Butter
Tomato & Basil Soup
Fricassée of Sole
with new potatoes & mange tout
Summer Pudding

Asparagus is of course the king of vegetables and should be treated with reverence. If you find this idea too fancy then just have it plain.

The combination of tomato and basil is to me absolutely fantastic, quite apart from the flavour the colours are so good. If I had half a chance there would be more recipes with them in this book but I was not allowed too many!

I love fish and a light fricassée makes expensive sole go a long way. At this time of year it is possible to buy the fine mange tout peas from Scotland.

Summer pudding is my favourite pudding, what more can I say.

Autumn

I have chosen a three-course meal here since all three are substantial.

The celebration of the vegetables and apples is balanced by the warming of winter in Cullen Skink. Brambles bring up the rear of the soft fruit season, not to mention rowan berries which make excellent jelly.

Cullen Skink
Chicken in the Pot
Caramelised Apple Tart

Depending on which meal this is for, the Skink can be lighter with the addition of more milk or water, or richer with lots of smoked fish and potato.

The chicken needs no extra vegetable and is a real Sunday lunch dish.

The apple tart can be served with just cream or cream with a little Drambuie folded through it, or even Drambuie ice cream.

Winter

Hearty warming food to be enjoyed over a long time since there is nothing much else to do!

We are fortunate with our natural larder of winter foods which can be livened up with a few colourful extras.

Scotch Broth
Winter Salad
Rabbit with Prunes
with Dauphinoise potatoes
and braised red cabbage
Crème Brulée

Scotch broth is possibly too much for a first course, if you think so then change it for a less powerful soup. The winter salad is a little fun. It is nice to have something raw to crunch on and at this time of year the colour and crunch are a welcome change.

The sweetness of the prunes in this dish really transcends the rabbit, don't let your prejudice stop you from trying it!

Crème Brulée is classic Aberdeenshire fare: lots of good cream and eggs.

Scottish Cheese

Cheese has made something of a comeback in Scotland and we now have a wide range of high quality cheeses. Many are handmade from unpasteurised milk, which allows the true flavours of the milk to develop as the cheese matures and ripens. The following list is by no means exhaustive; cheesemakers come and go. Some have also sadly been unable to keep up with the expense of having to make their cheese in sterile premises, in spite of cheese having been handmade in back kitchens for centuries.

Lanark Blue: Perhaps the best known Scottish cheese, made by Humphrey Errington in Ogcastle. It is mould ripened, semi-hard, made from unpasteurised ewes' milk.

Dunsyre Blue: The sister to the Lanark Blue, made the same way but from unpasteurised cows' milk.

Isle of Mull: Made on Sgriob-ruadh Farm on the island of Mull. A cloth-bound cheddar, handmade using unpasteurised cows' milk. The cheese is matured in 25kg (50lb) cylinders for up to 1 year.

Dunloppe: This is a traditional Ayrshire cheese, made to a recipe similar to that of cheddar. This one is made from pasteurised Friesian cows' milk, in a traditional cheesecloth wrapping.

Loch Arthur Farmhouse Cheese: This biodynamic cheese is made from the milk of Ayrshire cows. Aged up to 7 months.

Bonchester: John Curtis' Jersey herd produce the milk for this great cheese. The milk is unpasteurised and is mould ripened. It is a soft creamy cheese like Brie or Camembert.

Teviotdale: Similar to Bonchester, but made in large cylinders and lightly pressed.

Strathkinness: Rind-washed, made in 20kg (40lb) rounds developing Gruyère-like holes, this is the one I like to use for cooking, it is also excellent eaten on its own.

St Andrews: Modelled on Reblochon, rind-washed in 2.5kg (5lb) rounds.

Bishop Kennedy: The same as above, but washed in whisky.

Stichil: This Cheshire-style cheese is made from Jersey cows' milk.

Bonnet: A cheddar type made from unpasteurised goats' milk

Strathdon Blue: A blue cheese from Aberdeen made with unpasteurised milk.

Gigha Crottins: Both Arran and Gigha crottins are lovely white crumbly cylinders. Only made in the summer when the goats' milk is good.

There is now a wide range of high quality Scottish Cheeses

Glossary

Anchovy Essence Anchovy paste (USA)

Bake Blind This refers to cooking a lined pastry case from raw with no ingredients in it, usually by lining it with greaseproof paper and then filling it with dried beans. The case is then baked in a hot oven to cook the pastry, the beans and greaseproof paper are removed before the filling is added.

Bain Marie, or water bath; this is a large pan such as a roasting tin filled with water in which saucepans or bowls containing food are placed. This prevents direct heat being applied to the food, thus ensuring a low heat to prevent overcooking.

Batons A cut of vegetable like a matchstick.

Beurre Manié Equal amounts of flour and soft butter worked together to form a paste, added as a thickening agent to stews.

Blaeberry Also called whortleberry or bilberry or blueberry.

Blanch To plunge a food, usually vegetables, into boiling water briefly to enable you to remove the skin, as in tomatoes. For tomatoes; use firm but ripe tomatoes for this. Make a small criss-cross cut in the top of the fruit and cut out the core left behind by the stalk. Prepare a pan of simmering water and a bowl of ice cold water. Plunge the tomatoes first into the boiling water, leave for between 10 and 15 seconds depending on their size, then remove and put into cold water until they are cool. The skin will easily slip off.

Boiling Fowl Stewing fowl (USA).

Bramble Blackberry.

Caramelise To boil sugar and water together until they go brown.

Caster Sugar Granulated sugar (USA).

Clarified Butter The fat of the butter separated from the milk.

Cornflour Cornstarch (USA).

Double Cream Whipping cream (USA).

Egg Wash An egg well beaten used to brush over pastry before baking to give a glossy brown colour.

Flaked Almonds Slivered almonds (USA).

Fold In This is to incorporate two substances together such as cream and egg whites, to ensure that the air is not knocked out of the final mixture. Use either a plastic spatula or a large metal spoon, but not a wooden spoon.

Grilling In a professional kitchen a grill is a piece of equipment in which the heat source comes from below and you cook on it. A salamander has the heat above just like a grill in a domestic kitchen. A char grill is like a barbecue, it has bars and the heat is diffused through charcoal. Cooking meat like beef, venison or lamb under a domestic grill is not satisfactory, it is much better to cook on the stove in a heavy based pan, or put a char grill in your kitchen! Broil (USA).

Kippers The salted herring, introduced like so many of the methods of preserving fish by the Vikings, has in modern times become the kipper, which is a herring cleaned and split open, lightly brined and smoked for about 8 hours.

Knock Back To knead dough again until it is back to its original size.

Liaison A thickening for a sauce or soup or a type of sauce made from oil and egg yolk.

Mushroom Ketchup A sauce or essence from mushrooms.

Pinhead Oatmeal Irish oatmeal (USA).

Rashers Slices (USA).

Reduce To allow a liquid to simmer gently, thus evaporating the water and so reducing the quantity of liquid, which will then have a strong flavour.

Roulade A roll.

Rub In Spreading butter or fat onto the skin of a piece of meat or fish to be cooked. Also to use fingertips to combine butter or margarine with flour to make a shortbread or crumble mixture.

Saddle The backbone of rabbit, venison, hare or lamb.

Seasoning It is best to use freshly ground black pepper, salt should be rock or sea salt.

Self Raising Flour All-purpose flour with baking powder (USA).

Setting Point The temperature at which jam or marmalade will set. To test it take a small amount of jam and put it on a cold plate, if it firms up then the jam is ready to put into jars.

Single Cream Light cream (USA).

Strong Flour Flour high in gluten, good for making bread.

Wholemeal Flour Wholewheat flour (USA).

Wild Mushrooms Chanterelles, ceps or boletus or any other mushroom you can collect in the wild. Do be sure that you know what you are collecting. Some fungi can be poisonous. In France any chemist will tell you which of your freshly gathered fungi are edible! Sadly we are not so sophisticated here. You can also buy wild mushrooms from shops and from Strathspey Mushrooms Ltd, who provide excellent air-dried boletus. (See under Suppliers, p157.)

Recommended Suppliers

Whilst this list is by no means exhaustive, it provides a cross section of suppliers of some of the main ingredients found in this book. Most of them provide a mail-order service and their quality is of the highest.

Aberfeldy Watermill
Mill Street, Aberfeldy, Perthshire PH15 2BT
Tel: 01887 820803
Traditional oat producers.

The Big Cheese
22 Belmont Street, Aberdeen AB10 1JH
Good range of Scottish cheeses.

Eassie Asparagus
Sandy and Heather Pattullo
Eassie Farm, Eassie, Forfar DD8 1SG
Tel: 01307 840303
The best asparagus in the world!

Fletchers of Auchtermuchty
Nicola Fletcher
Reediehill, Auchtermuchty, Fife KY14 7HS
Tel: 01337 828369
Farmed venison products, mail order.

Heather Ale Ltd
Craigmill, Strathaven,
Lanarkshire ML10 6PB
Tel: 01357 529529
Suppliers of Fraoch Heather Ale.

Howgate Cheese
Kinfauns Home Farm, by Kinfauns Castle,
Kinfauns, Perthshire PH2 7JZ
Tel: 01738 443440
Farmhouse speciality cheesemakers.

Iain Mellis Cheesemonger
30A Victoria Street, Edinburgh EH1 2JW
Tel: 0131 226 6215
and
492 Great Western Road, Glasgow G12 8EW
Tel: 0141 339 8998
Superb range of Scottish cheeses, also by mail order.

Inverawe Smokehouses
Rosie Campbell Preston
Taynuilt, Argyll PA35 1HU
Tel: 01866 822446
Possibly the best smoked salmon in Scotland, excellent mail order, and many other products.

Inverloch Cheese Company
Leim Farm, Isle of Gigha, Argyll PA41 7AB
Tel: 01583 505209
Mail order suppliers of Gigha goats' cheese crottins.

Keracher Fishmonger
49 Scott Street, Perth PH2 8JN
Tel: 01738 623519
Wide variety of fresh fish.

Loch Fyne Oysters
(Shop & Oyster Bar)
Clachan, Cairndow, Argyll PA26 8BL
Tel: 01499 600236
Superb fresh oysters, with mail order service.

Macbeth the Butcher

Mike Gibson
11 Tolbooth Street, Forres, Moray IB36 0PH
Tel: 01309 672254
Superb quality beef from Highland Aberdeen Angus
and other breeds of cattle, mail order.

Macdonald's Smoked Produce

Glenuig, Lochailort, Ardnamurchan
Inverness-shire PH38 4NG
Tel: 01687 470266
Winner of numerous food awards. Excellent smoked
cheese, salmon and haggis, among other exotic items.

MacSween Haggis Specialist

Dryden Road, Bilston Glen, Loanhead
Edinburgh EH20 9LZ
Tel: 0131 440 2555
Haggis makers, mail order.

Ramsay of Carluke

Wellriggs, 22 Mount Stewart Street,
Carluke ML8 5ED
Tel: 01555 772277
Traditional bacon curers, mail order service.

Rannoch Smokery

Leo and Sarah Barclay
Kinloch Rannoch, near Pitlochry,
Perthshire PH16 5QD
Tel: 01882 632344
Suppliers of the only smoked wild venison in
Scotland, as well as fresh venison steaks. They also
smoke chicken, duck, grouse and pheasant (in
season).

Scotherbs

Kingswell, Longforgen,
near Dundee DD2 5HJ
Tel: 01382 360642
Mail order cut fresh herbs all year round.

Scotland's Larder

Christopher Trotter
Upper Largo, Leven, Fife KY8 6EA
Tel: 01333 360414
A unique centre providing an insight into quality
Scottish food. The shop covers a wide variety of
fresh seasonal produce. Regular demonstrations and
seasonal dinners represent the best of Scottish food.
The restaurant offers the full spectrum of Scottish
food as well as Friday and Saturday dinner menus
where you can eat many of the dishes in this book.
Mail order service and Scottish hampers.

The Scottish Gourmet

Thistle Mill, Station Road, Biggar ML12 6LP
Tel: 0500 340640
Mail order food club.

Strathspey Mushrooms

Unit 12, Dalfaber Industrial Estate, Dalfaber
Road, Aviemore, Inverness-shire PH22 1PY
Tel: 01479 810583
Dried wild mushrooms from Speyside.

Valvona & Crolla

19 Elm Row, Edinburgh EH7 4AA
Tel: 0131 556 6066
Top quality delicatessen.

Weights & Measures

It is important to use either metric or imperial measurements when following recipes, do not mix them. Conversions given are not exact equivalents, but have been rounded up or down for convenience; any slight variations have been taken into account, and should not adversely affect the recipes.

Liquid Conversions

METRIC	IMPERIAL	US
30ml	1fl oz	⅛ cup
60ml	2fl oz	¼ cup
125ml	4fl oz	½ cup
150ml	5fl oz (¼ pint)	⅔ cup
250ml	8fl oz	1 cup (½ pint)
300ml	10fl oz (½ pint)	1¼ cups
500ml	16fl oz	2 cups (1 pint)
600ml	1 pint (20fl oz)	2½ cups
1 litre	1³/₄ pints	1qt (4 cups)
1.25 litres	2 pints (1qt)	1¼qts
2 litres	3¹/₄ pints	2qts

Solid Weight Conversions

METRIC	IMPERIAL
15g	¹/₂oz
25g	1oz
50g	2oz
125g	4oz (¹/₄lb)
175g	6oz
250g	8oz (¹/₂lb)
350g	12oz (³/₄lb)
500g	1lb

Level Spoon Sizes

METRIC	IMPERIAL
5ml	1tsp
10ml	1dsp
15ml	1tbsp

Bibliography

Below is a list of books that I have used or which have inspired me. Of the modern ones, Sybil Kapoor's *Modern British Food* is particularly exciting.

Brown, Catherine, *Broth to Bannocks,* John Murray Ltd, London, 1990.

Brown, Catherine, *Taste of Scotland Chef's Manual,* 1985.

Castlemain, *Lady Castlemain's Cook Book,* (original collection 1712), The Molendinar Press, Glasgow, 1976.

Fitzgibbon, Theodora, *Traditional Scottish Cookery,* Fontana paperbacks, 1980.

Fitzgibbon, Theodora, *A Taste of Scotland,* Pan Books, London, 1971.

Guerard, Michel, *La Cuisine Gourmand,* Macmillan, London, 1978.

Kapoor, Sybil, *Modern British Food,* Penguin Books, 1996.

Maclean, *Lady Maclean's Cook Book,* Collins, 1975.

Verge, Roger, *Cuisine of the Sun,* Macmillan, London, 1979.

Index